GODS
MEN & MONSTERS
from the Greek Myths

HELIOS,
THE SUN

HERA,
QUEEN OF HEAVEN

ZEUS,
LORD OF OLYMPUS

HESTIA,
GODDESS OF THE
HOME

IRIS,
MESSENGER OF
HERA

HEPHAESTUS,
THE SMITH GOD

ATHENE,
GODDESS OF
WISDOM

DIONYSUS,
GOD OF WINE

DEMETER,
GODDESS OF AGRICULTURE

APOLLO,
GOD OF MUSIC

POSEIDON,
GOD OF THE SEA

APHRODITE,
GODDESS OF LOVE

EROS,
GOD OF LOVE

GODS MEN & MONSTERS

from the Greek Myths

ILLUSTRATIONS BY GIOVANNI CASELLI   TEXT BY MICHAEL GIBSON

SCHOCKEN BOOKS

NEW YORK

ARES,
GOD OF WAR

PAN,
GOD OF THE COUNTRYSIDE

ARTEMIS,
GODDESS OF THE HUNT

HERMES,
MESSENGER
OF THE GODS

CHARON,
THE FERRYMAN

CERBERUS,
THE WATCHDOG
OF HADES

HADES,
LORD OF THE UNDERWORLD

First American edition published by Schocken Books 1982

10 9 8 7 6   87 88 89

Library of Congress Cataloging in Publication Data

Gibson, Michael.
  Gods, men & monsters from the Greek myths.

(World mythologies series)
Includes index.
  Summary: A collection of myths relating the exploits and adventures of the gods and heroes of ancient Greece.
  1. Mythology, Greek. [1. Mythology, Greek] I. Caselli, Giovanni, fl. 1976–   ill.
II. Title. III. Title: Gods, men and monsters from the Greek myths.
BL782.G53   1982   292′.13
81–14542
AACR2

Manufactured in Italy by Grafiche Editoriali Padane SpA
ISBN 0-8052-3793-3

THE AUTHOR

Michael Gibson has worked for many years as an editor and has written over twenty children's books himself. The Greek myths and legends have always fascinated him, but took on a new meaning after he visited and came to know the places where so many of the stories are set. He has studied and qualified as a spare-time archaeologist.

THE ARTIST

Giovanni Caselli is a Florentine living in London. Since the early 1960s he has been involved in researching and preparing a series of paintings showing reconstructions of life in the past. As a student of archaeology and anthropology he has carried out extensive field researches in Italy.

Contents

The world of the gods

Greece is a land of many contrasts. It has flat plains, foothills and mountain ranges. In places along its jagged coastline are high cliffs and the surrounding seas are sprinkled with islands both large and small, some inhabited and some not. The lower-lying lands are fertile, and on the slopes are vineyards. In spring in the wilder places the ground is ablaze with wild flowers, which grow for some way up the mountains, contrasting with the grey-green leaves of the herbs which also flourish there. However, the brilliant colours last only for a short while before the heat of the summer sun makes the flowers vanish as quickly as they came. Then the only vegetation outside the more sheltered valleys consists of clumps of small, stunted pines and scrub. In winter there is snow on the mountain peaks.

In ancient times, particularly on the higher ground, the country was much more wooded and less barren than it is today. Many centuries of close cropping by the herds of long-eared goats and sheep kept by peasant farmers have destroyed sapling trees and young shrubs. Without these, there were no long roots to help bind the soil together when it dried out in the burning summer sun and over the years it became thin and powdery and was blown away. The rocks, never far below the surface, were exposed and in the scanty soil left in the cracks only the toughest grasses and the herbs which grow best in these poor conditions could survive. At the time of the legends, however, none of this had happened and woods and forests were plentiful.

The coast is probably much the same as it was in the old days. As was perhaps to be expected in a land with so many natural harbours, the ancient Greeks were excellent sailors. Their influence spread well beyond the mainland of Greece and its surrounding islands to many of the other Mediterranean countries, particularly the eastern ones. This is reflected in the legends, many of which mention voyages to other lands. Greece itself, though one country overall, was divided into many city-states, each with its own king and queen and ruling families. The city-states sometimes combined in a common cause, as many did in the war against Troy, and in the long siege that followed it. At other times there was often intense rivalry between different states or, at the very least, a great sense of independence. Many states were separated from their neighbours by high mountain ranges, which made communication far from easy.

The isolation of one state from another was one reason why the stories the people told of the gods and mortals varied from place to place. They were not written down until long afterwards, but were passed from one generation to another by word of mouth. Each storyteller gave his own version, perhaps elaborating on it if he had the imagination to do so. Gradually one part of the country would accept a particular account, but it might differ greatly from the story established in another place. Few people travelled far enough around the country to compare the different versions. It was not until between six and seven hundred years before the birth of Christ, and about four hundred years after Troy had fallen, that the poet Homer and a few other Greek writers collected the stories together. Homer wrote two great narrative poems about the old heroes, the *Iliad*, which tells the story of the siege of Troy, and the *Odyssey*, which is the story of Odysseus's journey home after the battle.

In the folk legends of most countries there is some element of truth, and this is probably true of Greece also. Archaeologists have unearthed many objects that seem to have a link with some of the tales. Perhaps the most famous example of this occurred in the case of the German businessman Heinrich Schliemann. As a boy, his favourite stories were the old legends of Greece. He believed very strongly that many of them were based on fact. When he grew up he went into business so that he could make enough money to realize the dream that had always been at the forefront of his mind – to find the ancient city of Troy. He was middle-aged by the time he actually started excavating at what he believed to be the right place, but he had spent the years studying the texts of the stories in great detail. By following every clue he could find in them he did indeed find the site of Troy – much to the amazement of the professional archaeologists of the time, who had ridiculed his theories. In fact, through lack of training and skilled help, he dug right through the Troy described in the works of Homer, and found underneath the remains of an even older city. Later, amongst other discoveries, he unearthed the old city of Mycenae, home of the Greek king Agamemnon, following clues from the legends in the same way.

Like many early peoples, the Greeks did not believe in only one god. They had many gods and goddesses, some of which they associated with the great forces of nature, or with human emotions. Thus Poseidon was the god of the sea, and Aphrodite the goddess of love. Before a battle the Greeks would ask Ares, god of war, for his help. Other gods and goddesses were chosen to represent practical and leisure activities: Hestia was the goddess of the home, Demeter the goddess of harvests, Apollo the god of music and Athene the goddess of the arts, especially spinning and weaving, and of wisdom. Some gods were given a number of attributes: Apollo, for instance, was responsible not only for music, but for archery, medicine and prophecy. Oracles, special shrines where priests and priestesses interpreted the messages of the gods, were found in many places, the most famous being the oracle of Apollo at Delphi. Both gods and goddesses were adopted as patron of a particular city or state, as Athene was for Athens. Over all the gods ruled Zeus and his wife Hera, who watched everything that happened from the heights of Mount Olympus – a mountain in northern Greece.

In time, perhaps because the ancient Greeks wished to feel that the gods they worshipped were not too remote from themselves, the gods were described in the legends as mixing freely with mortals in their adventures. However, there were strict rules as to what mortals might or might not do. For example, they could never be allowed to challenge a god's supremecy; the few who tried to do so usually regretted it, for the gods were jealous and vengeful.

Another way in which the Greeks tried to make the all-powerful gods seem less austere was to give them human weaknesses. Zeus – from whom, as the absolute ruler, one would expect dignified, responsible behaviour at all times – could never resist the attractions of a pretty girl, much to the annoyance of his wife Hera. The gods ruled, above all, by jealousy and by their desire for revenge. Again and again in the Greek legends, these two passions are the driving forces behind the immortals' actions.

Some of the horrifying deeds described in the legends probably had their origins in stories which came from outside Greece. Some of the legends themselves seem to come from an even earlier time and from much further east, for the same plots are found there, though the characters are different. If this is true, the Greeks probably adapted stories brought by invaders, or heard in other lands, to fit their own ritual practices, the true meanings of which had been forgotten. Some of the stories came from countries that were still much more primitive than Greece, places where human life was cheap and torture and other cruelties were considered a normal part of life. Even among the Greeks themselves human sacrifice was not unknown and animal sacrifice was a common occurrence.

Besides the gods, there are a number of other mythical creatures in the Greek legends. There were, for example, the centaurs, half man and half horse, the satyrs, half man and half goat, and the sea and wood nymphs, the nereids and the dryads. These strange creatures lived on earth but, like the gods, they had special powers. So, too, did the marvellous monsters against which both gods and mortals fought, usually successfully. Typhon, who had one hundred serpent heads, and Echidna, half woman and half serpent, produced many of the terrifying monsters found in the stories that follow. There was Orthrus, against which Hercules fought; Cerberus, the hideous three-headed hound which guarded the gates of Hades; the Chimaera, half goat and half lion, with the tail of a serpent; the terrible Sphinx of Thebes who strangled her victims; the Hydra with its writhing snake heads; and the man-eating Nemean lion.

The monsters represented the forces of evil, and the suppression of evil is a strong theme throughout the stories. Often the heroes tackled the most daunting tasks single-handed for no better reason than to assert the triumph of good. If they were brave and resourceful, there was a strong chance that they would receive help from a god at the crucial moment.

The gods that the Greeks worshipped and that play a major part in the legends are known as the New Gods. But they did not suddenly appear from nowhere. Their history goes back to the beginning of time, before the earth was created. First there was Chaos, a state which cannot be defined clearly, for it was a whirling mass of nothing, without shape or form. From Chaos, Mother Earth emerged. Her son Uranus fashioned the earth in the form in which we know it, and made the flowers, trees, animals and birds. We know little about him as an individual.

Mother Earth also gave birth to three-headed giants and to the one-eyed Cyclopes, whose sons became workers in the forge of Hephaestus, the smith god. The Cyclopes did not find favour with Uranus and he cast them down to the Underworld, greatly angering Mother Earth. However, she bore Uranus twelve children, six sons and six daughters, who became the Titans. Of these old gods, Oceanus, Cronus and Rhea appear with some frequency in the myths of the immortals.

Mother Earth did not forget the harsh treatment that Uranus had given her first children. She persuaded the Titans to seek their revenge. Cronus, the youngest of the twelve, was the leader. He attacked Uranus with a flint scythe while he slept. Three drops of the blood from Uranus's wounds fell on Mother Earth and these became the terrible Furies, who lived in the Underworld. From that time, Cronus ruled the Titans, with Rhea as his wife. But though he was now all-powerful, his mind was not easy. When Uranus was dying, he had prophesied that one of Cronus's sons would one day overthrow him and take his place. To guard against this, Cronus decided to destroy his children and for five years running, as Rhea bore him sons and daughters, he snatched them from her arms and swallowed them before they opened their eyes.

This, of course, did not please Rhea at all and when she knew that a sixth child was to be born, she went secretly to Mount Lycaeum in the district of central Greece known as Arcadia. It was there that the baby Zeus was born. Rhea left him hidden safely in a cave, in the care of the nymphs Adrasteia, Io and Amaltheia. The new gods had arrived.

The new gods~Zeus and Hera

When the era of the new gods began with the survival of the infant Zeus, the Titans did not simply vanish overnight. A few of them, with their sons and daughters, lived on into the new age. Before this, however, there were old scores to settle and wrongs to be righted.

When Cronus found out what Rhea had done with her new child, he was furiously angry and at once ordered a thorough search to be made. To drown the sounds of the baby's crying, the nymphs arranged for a great noise to be made whenever the searchers came near his hiding place: gongs were beaten, swords clashed on shields and men shouted to one another as if a loud argument was in progress. To baffle Cronus still further, Zeus was taken from the cave and hung in his cradle from the branches of a tree, so that he was neither on the earth nor in the sky nor in the sea. However, the search continued and Rhea knew that unless she took further action, sooner or later her child would be discovered. Wrapping a large stone in swaddling clothes, she presented it to Cronus as her son – and he promptly swallowed it as he had his five real children.

Cronus now thought he was safe, and under the

care of the kindly nymphs, Zeus grew to manhood. From time to time Rhea visited him in the cave and told him what had happened to his brothers and sisters. As he grew older, he determined to rescue them. Together, Zeus and Rhea went to Metis, a wise Titaness who had no love for Cronus, and she suggested a plan.

Cronus had never seen his son, so when Rhea introduced a young cup-bearer to him, praising him highly, Cronus was easily persuaded to employ him. As soon as he was a trusted servant, Zeus mixed a potion and poured it into his father's drinking cup. Its effect was to make Cronus violently sick. Out of his mouth, quite unharmed, came Hades, Poseidon, Demeter, Hera and Hestia, the two sons and three daughters whom Cronus had swallowed. Out, too, came the stone which Rhea had given him instead of the infant Zeus. It fell to earth at the sacred shrine of Delphi, where it became an object of veneration and where it can be seen even to this day.

Now that they were free, Poseidon and Hades were eager to take their revenge. They persuaded Zeus to lead them against those Titans who supported the now ageing Cronus. The leader of the Titan army, and Cronus's deputy, was a mighty god named Atlas.

The war between the old and the new gods was long and bitter. At last Zeus was advised to seek the help of the one-eyed Cyclopes, who had been imprisoned all this while in the Underworld. Zeus journeyed there to release them and in gratitude they gave presents to the three sons of Cronus: to Zeus a thunderbolt, which was to become his most characteristic weapon; to Hades a helmet which made him invisible whenever he wore it; to Poseidon a trident. Armed with these weapons, the three found Cronus alone. Hades, wearing his helmet, was able to steal Cronus's weapons without being seen. Just as Cronus discovered they were gone, Poseidon threatened him with his three-pronged trident and Zeus crept up behind to strike him down with a thunderbolt. The blow killed Cronus instantly.

Discouraged by the death of the god for whom they had fought so long, the remaining Titans lost heart. A deadly rain of rocks was hurled at them by the Cyclopes and they were swiftly defeated. All but two were banished to Tartarus, the part of the Underworld where people suffered eternal torment. Cronus was allowed to live in the happier environment of the Elysian Fields, but Atlas, the war leader, was condemned to atone for his deeds by holding the weight of the heavens on his massive shoulders for evermore.

Zeus's mind now turned to other things and his foremost task was the creation of mankind. First, he made the men of the Golden Age, who lived in Paradise. They laughed and sang all day and the bounty of the earth was provided for them to eat: fruit from the trees, honey from the wild bees, berries and nuts from shady thickets and milk from the goats and sheep. The men did no work and their lives were completely happy. Eventually the men grew old and died, but afterwards their spirits roamed the earth, keeping watch over the welfare of later generations.

The next creations were the men of the Silver Age. They, unlike the first men, were not far removed from the lowest animals. They were brutish and dull-witted, and refused to make sacrifices to their creators as they had been taught. Instead, they quarrelled among themselves. Zeus, realizing that they would never improve, destroyed them all with little regret.

The next men he created, the men of the Bronze Age, were more intelligent, but otherwise little better. They used their minds not to create useful and beautiful things but solely for the design and manufacture of weapons of war. With these they fought each other until they, too, were all dead and were sent to dwell forever in the Underworld.

Zeus became discouraged. He wondered whether the human race was a good idea after all, and whether it was worth persevering. Eventually, he decided that he would try once again. This time he created the men of the Heroic Age, many of whom were to become the heroes of the legends told in later times. Zeus called on the help of a good and wise Titan to form the heroes and the story of how Prometheus befriended man against Zeus's orders is told later in the book.

Olympus, where the immortals lived, was thought to be the highest mountain in the world. Of those who gathered there, Zeus, Hermes, Poseidon, Hephaestus, Ares and Apollo were the greatest gods and Athene, Hera, Artemis, Aphrodite, Hestia and Demeter the most revered of the goddesses. Under the sovereignty of Zeus, these twelve were of the highest rank; others, such as Helios, Leto, Dionysus and Themis were next in importance. Pan, the shepherd god, was associated more with the countryside than with Olympus. Hades, Zeus's brother, would certainly have been an addition to the twelve principal

gods, but he rarely if ever came to their mountain home. He was content to live in his kingdom far beneath the earth, ruling over the shades of the dead in the Underworld.

Life on Olympus was good. The gods spent a good deal of time in the banqueting halls, feasting on the flesh of sacrifices made to them by mortals on the earth below and drinking nectar from golden goblets filled to the brim by lesser gods and goddesses such as Hebe and Ganymede, who played the role of courtiers. While they ate and drank, Apollo would fill the air with music from his lyre and the nine Muses would sing more sweetly than any mortal could imagine.

Often, however, one or other of the gods would be absent from the revelry, for they loved nothing better than to travel to earth and play a part in the lives of men. Many of the mortal heroes would have met untimely deaths if a god or goddess had not been watching over them and giving help when it was needed. In these adventures, the gods often took risks. However, the fact that they were immortal gave them great advantages: they could be wounded by a sword or spear, but the wounds quickly healed, for ichor, a fluid with remarkable qualities, flowed in their veins instead of blood; and they could, of course, change themselves at will into another form in order to achieve their purpose. Normally, however, the gods took human form so that they could move about undetected.

Though Zeus was supreme among the gods, even he was subject to the guidance of Destiny, the fount of all wisdom. Destiny's wise counselling kept order in the universe. Through Destiny, Zeus saw everything and knew everything. Zeus could hand out swift justice to wrongdoers, but he could also be compassionate and protect the weak, the poor and the ignorant. The ancient Greeks worshipped him as god of the sky and lord of the winds, rain and thunder, and Zeus

spoke to them either in his own person or through the oracle of Apollo at Delphi.

Hera became Zeus's wife, but she was not the first or the only one. The first was Metis the Titan. Next came Themis, a daughter of Uranus who gave birth to Peace, Justice and finally, to the Fates. These daughters of the night chose for each mortal the course his life would take. Themis remained in Olympus, even in the days of Hera, for Zeus valued her judgement on many matters and used to consult her about problems which troubled him. Hera did not seem to mind.

Two other wives followed Themis. Mnemosyne bore Zeus nine daughters, the Muses. Each one dedicated herself to a different art, though they were all gifted in music. At one time their supremacy in song was challenged by the nine daughters of Pierus, king of Emanthia in Macedonia. These unfortunate women were turned into magpies for daring to question who was best at singing. Finally, there was Eurynome, who bore Zeus the three Graces.

At one time Zeus grew too proud of his power over the other gods and his haughtiness made them resentful. A number of them, encouraged by Hera (who was annoyed with Zeus for neglecting her), thought that he needed to be taught a lesson. They siezed him and bound him with ropes, tied in a hundred knots. Helpless, he raged at them, but they only laughed mockingly. They discussed in front of him which god should be his successor, and he realized that unless something was done he would be supplanted, just as he had supplanted his father.

However, while Zeus struggled vainly to free himself, others became concerned at the prospect of yet another war among the gods. Among these was the sea nymph Thetis. She took swift action and brought the hundred-handed giant Briareus, a son of Uranus, to the spot where Zeus lay, fuming with anger. With each of his

hundred hands the giant untied one knot. In no time the mightiest of the gods was free once more and thirsting for revenge. Poseidon and Apollo, who had been two of the leaders in the plot, were sent far across the sea to Asia Minor to work for a while for King Laomedon, building the walls of Troy. Hera received more extreme punishment; she was hung from the sky with a heavy bronze anvil suspended from each ankle until all the other gods had sworn solemn oaths that they would never again rebel.

Hera and Zeus made a strange couple, for they fought and quarrelled most of the time. Generally Zeus was at fault, for though he respected his wife in many ways, he was constantly scheming to deceive her and go off adventuring on his own. She almost always found out what he was doing but, though she would remonstrate with him, she was careful never to go beyond a certain point. His temper was uncertain and she had good reason to know how violent he could be.

After her strange rebirth, Hera had been

brought up in Arcadia, and it was there that Zeus came looking for her when his wife Eurynome had gone. It was winter and there was snow on the ground. Zeus managed to win Hera's pity and her love by disguising himself as a distressed, half-frozen cuckoo, which she picked up and warmed in her arms. His attraction for her did not seem to decrease when he resumed his normal form. They planned a wedding and Mount Olympus was filled with rejoicing and celebration when the news reached the other gods.

Presents were showered on the couple. Mother Earth gave Hera a tree which bore golden apples. It was planted in a garden on the side of Mount Atlas, close to where Atlas the Titan held the world on his shoulders. In due course Ares, the god of war, Hephaestus, the smith god, and Hebe were born to Hera. These were Zeus's only children by Hera. Hebe spent her life as a handmaiden to the other gods, so little can be told about her, though her brothers led more eventful existences.

The
Family of
the Gods

Zeus's constant unfaithfulness to Hera is difficult to explain, for she was young and certainly beautiful. Perhaps she was rather severe, taking her place as queen of the gods too seriously. Hera took great care always to appear at her best. Each year she went to bathe in the magic waters of the spring at Nauplia on the coast of Greece, for they renewed her youth. After bathing, she would anoint her body with sweetly-scented oils before returning to her husband on Olympus. She remained faithful to Zeus though she would not have lacked suitors had she wished for them. One man, Ixion, a king of Thessaly, did try to court her, but was quickly thwarted by Zeus and sent to eternal punishment in Tartarus for his presumption.

Once, when Zeus's adventures became too much for her, she left him and returned to the island of Euboea, where she had spent her very early years before her time in Arcadia. Zeus tried every way he could think of to get her back, but she remained firm. Then he thought of a plan which he was fairly sure would work, for he knew from experience how jealous Hera could be.

He had a statue made in the shape of a beautiful girl. He dressed it in the finest robes of spun gold, and he crowned the flaxen hair with a coronet of pearls. He placed the statue in a golden chariot and had it driven from place to place about the island while heralds proclaimed that it was the bride-to-be of the ruler of the gods. In a fury, Hera rushed at the chariot and tore the clothes from the statue, only to find that she had been tricked. However, her true feelings for Zeus had been all too plainly shown. She had no option but to return, rather shamefacedly, to Olympus.

The strange story of how Zeus alone gave birth to Athene will be told later. Hera was more angered by the incident than by his usual escapades. Jealous of the strange power which had been given to him, she wished for it herself and called Mother Earth and the Titans in Tartarus to her aid. In due course her wish was granted. But instead of a handsome son, it was the monster Typhon that she brought into the world.

Hera was quite ruthless with her rivals, and with any women whom she thought might be a danger to her. Antigone, daughter of Laomedon of Troy, was heard to boast that her hair was finer and more silky by far than that of the goddess, and for this foolishness it was promptly turned into a tangled nest of writhing serpents. On another occasion, the daughters of Proetus, king of Argos, spoke contemptuously of the beauty of a statue of Hera. Hera afflicted them with madness to teach them better manners. Only when a famous prophet intervened on their behalf did the goddess relent and restore them to their former selves.

When not provoked by Zeus, Hera could be wise and compassionate. She had a great liking for the brave and noble among the mortals and helped many of them when they were in trouble. It was her guiding hand, for example, which saw Jason safely through his long and perilous voyage in search of the golden fleece.

Zeus's behaviour, when he managed to evade Hera's watchful eye, was frequently disgraceful. On one occasion Zeus looked down from Olympus and saw Io, daughter of Inachus, a ruler of Argos. Io was very beautiful and Zeus fell in love with her at once. He visited her and they talked for a while, but they were careless and Hera spied them out. On seeing Hera draw near, Zeus turned Io into a white cow and pretended that the cow was one of a herd which was grazing nearby. But Hera was not deceived. She acted as though she thought that the cow was a present for her and thanked Zeus profusely. He had no choice but to leave it and return with her to Olympus.

Next day he slipped away and returned to Argos, intending to restore Io to her real self and hide her, but he found to his annoyance that Hera had summoned a hundred-eyed monster named Argus to guard the cow. Zeus dared not use one of his thunderbolts to kill the monster, as this would have made his own guilt obvious, so he sent the smooth-tongued Hermes to deal with it for him. Hermes sat with Argus throughout the night, unfolding a long, sad saga which at first held the monster enthralled. After many hours, the monster dozed, and finally it slept. At once Hermes sprang up and with one blow from his sword cut Argus's head from its body.

The terrified Io took flight and when they looked for her she was gone beyond recall. She wandered for many months, northward through Greece and round the eastern Mediterranean, over mountains and burning deserts, until she reached the land of Egypt. There, restored to human form, she bore Zeus's child, a son who was to become the first Pharaoh to rule the kingdom of the Nile.

Hades, Lord of the Underworld

The name Hades can lead to some confusion, for it was used by the ancient Greeks both for the god who ruled the Underworld and for the kingdom of the Underworld itself. Though it was the world of the dead, the Greek Hades was not like the later idea of hell, a place where the damned go to suffer eternal torment. It was a place where all the dead – good or bad – journeyed, guided there by the messenger god Hermes. Only when they arrived was their fate decided. Some, particularly those who had offended the gods, did suffer, but those who had been good and wise and kind, and those who had achieved brave deeds, could lead an afterlife of great happiness. Over all such matters ruled the god Hades, a stern but at the same time always just king.

Hades himself does not feature strongly in Greek legends because once he had been established as Lord of the Underworld, he seldom left it. Once or twice, when a nymph caught his fancy, he ventured out in his chariot with its sinister-looking black horses, and on one brief visit to earth he seized Demeter's daughter Persephone. But generally, Hades stayed out of sight in his own kingdom.

The kingdom of Hades, however, plays a most important part in Greek legends. Many of the Greek heroes, together with other gods, visited it for one reason or another while they were still living. A favourite task for a god to set a mortal was to go to Hades and bring back some object or token of the visit. It needed great ingenuity (or the help of a magic spell) for a mortal to get both into Hades and out again.

In the very early days, it was believed that Hades lay far to the west, beyond the horizon where the river Oceanus, which encircled the earth, began. Later, some stories contained descriptions of dark caverns and long, gloomy passages which led down to the Underworld from districts on the mainland of Greece such as Thesprotia in the west or from across the Aegean Sea in Asia Minor. Wherever they entered, the dead could always rely on Hermes to show them the way.

When a dead person was buried, a small coin called an *obol* would be placed in his mouth. Uttering comforting words – if he felt that they were deserved – Hermes then led the shade of the dead person away from his sorrowing relatives, down, down, deep beneath the earth to the threshold of Hades. Here they had to halt, for the Underworld was bounded by rivers on all sides. These were slow, sluggish streams running through gloomy tunnels which opened out only occasionally to a cavern where a crossing could be made. The Styx was the river that bordered the part of Hades called Tartarus on its western side, and its tributaries – the Acheron and four others – encircled the rest.

The crossing was usually made over the Styx, but not if the *obol* had been forgotten or lost, nor if the shade was too poor to pay it. In that event, he would be left to wait forever without hope on the bank, for the Styx had a ferryman who demanded a toll from everyone who used his boat. This boatman was the rough and surly Charon. When the *obol* had been paid, he would grudgingly take the shade across. Hades had instructed him, threatening him with heavy punishment if he disobeyed, not to carry any living person, however good their reasons might seem for crossing the river. One or two, greatly daring, did occasionally manage to evade Charon, or persuade him to make an exception to his rule.

Hermes left his charge on the banks of the Styx. The shade would then board the boat, Charon's oars would dip silently into the murky waters and the boat would gradually draw away from the shore, taking its passengers away from the land of the living for ever. On the farther bank was the monstrous, three-headed dog, Cerberus. In spite of his terrifying appearance, Cerberus meant no harm to the shades of the dead as they stepped from Charon's boat. His duty was to bar the way if, at a later time, they tried to recross the Styx to escape back to the world above. He also guarded the gates against unauthorized visitors.

Once he had landed, the shade had to cross the Plain of Asphodel. This was a place of mists and shadowy trees, with sad, weeping branches which brushed the ground and sighed dismally in the wind that blew continuously across the flat, grey land. Here the less fortunate mortals – those with no special claim to make when they were judged – spent eternity, drifting aimlessly about. They suffered no special torment, except boredom, but most would gladly have escaped if they could.

Beyond the Plain of Asphodel lay the green meadows of Erebus and the Pool of Lethe, where the common dead came to drink. Anyone who tasted the waters of Lethe immediately forgot their past life in the world above, so the common shades were without even memories to sustain them. Beyond rose the towers of the splendid palace of Hades, but none of the dead were privileged to pass through its wide, metal-studded door. Only visiting gods from Olympus and the lesser gods of the Underworld itself were allowed to cross the threshold, together with the very few who, from time to time, were summoned before the king of the Underworld and his queen, Persephone.

Before they reached the borders of the palace grounds, the shades halted to await judgement on their past live. The judges were Minos, Rhadamanthus and Aeacus, chosen because of their great wisdom and because of the worthy lives they had led on earth. Every day the newly dead were brought before them, perhaps trembling if they had led a wicked life, perhaps calm and silent, indifferent to their fate.

After they had been judged, the shades were taken down one of three paths. The first led back to the Plain of Asphodel. This path was well worn: few could convince the judges that they had special claims for other treatment, and so many had to stay eternally in the dismal surroundings where night and day merged into eternal twilight. A few – the great heroes, or those who had pleased the gods with sacrifices or a service rendered at the cost of their own lives – would be more lucky. Awaiting them, at the end of the second path, were the Elysian Fields.

Here, the sun shone and the only clouds in the blue sky were white and fleecy. Birds sang among the trees, most noticeably in the branches of the tall, white poplar which had once been the daughter of the god Oceanus. The clearings were always full of the sound of happy music played on the pipes and the lyre, and there was always dancing. Here there was no night, for the shades needed no rest. Banquets were held whenever the revellers were in the mood for one. Wine flowed, but no one suffered afterwards, for it was impossible to drink too much. Great dishes of grapes and pomegranates, flowing with the sweetest juice, were served at the end of each banquet.

Those fortunate enough to reach the Elysian Fields enjoyed a further privilege which the shades on the dreary Plain of Asphodel would have valued above everything else: they could, if they wished, return to earth. In fact their new life was so happy that very few chose to leave it, even for a short time.

The wise judge Rhadamanthus ruled over the Elysian Fields, or Elysium as it was sometimes called. One of his subjects was the Titan, Cronus. It may seem strange that Rhadamanthus had accepted Cronus for Elysium, for he had been a cruel and jealous god. However, some of the older and greater early gods, including Cronus, were automatically entitled to live in Elysium when they were supplanted – for gods cannot be said to die. There are no records that Cronus disturbed the happiness of others in Elysium, nor that his behaviour was different from that of a kindly old gentleman who, though rumour said he had been wild in his youth, was content to rest with his memories.

The third path along which the judges might send the dead led to Tartarus, the land bordered on one side by the River Styx. (In some versions, the name Tartarus is used for the whole of Hades.) Its entrance was a vast, bronze gate, which was kept always firmly locked from inside, opening only to admit the new dead. Tartarus was similar to the hell of the later Christian faith, a place of eternal punishment and damnation, reserved for the wicked and for those who had defied or angered the gods. Their cries of anguish echoed ceaselessly back from the high, triple walls which surrounded them, and no one was ever known to escape.

Of all those condemned forever to Tartarus, perhaps the most famous were the Titans, the old gods that Zeus and his brothers and sisters had replaced. Only Cronus lived in Elysium; the other supplanted gods were doomed to suffer for

eternity. Another resident was Tantalus, who had killed his young son Pelops and served his flesh to the gods to see if they could distinguish it from that of an animal. The gods found out what he had done, and Pelops was restored to life – though not before one of his shoulders had been eaten. He lived the rest of his life with an ivory shoulder, and Tantalus was banished at once to Hades. As a punishment, he was suspended from a fruit tree over a lake of clear water. He was constantly hungry and thirsty, but whenever he tried to reach out for some fruit, it shrank just out of his reach; and when he bent down to drink, the water receded, too. The word 'tantalize' comes from his sufferings.

Another sufferer was the giant Tityus, who had attacked Leto, the mother of Apollo and Artemis while she was praying at the sacred shrine of Delphi. Her son and daughter had saved her by riddling the giant with arrows, and in Tartarus, Tityus was spreadeagled on the ground, held fast by ropes, while vultures pecked at him with their cruel, curved beaks.

Sisyphus, one-time king of Corinth, had chained up Death when it came to claim him. For a long time no one died on earth, and it was not until Ares was sent to unleash Death again, that Hades's kingdom returned to normal. For this, and other crimes, Sisyphus was in Tartarus, condemned forever to push a large boulder to the summit of a hill. As soon as he reached the top, the boulder immediately rolled down and Sisyphus had to start all over again. Nearby was Ixion from Thessaly, bound to a spinning, fiery wheel because he had dared to woo Hera, the wife of Zeus. Zeus had formed a cloud into the image of his wife to deceive Ixion. It worked so well that in time it bore to him the centaurs, strange creatures which were half man, half horse. Ixion's sin, though unsuccessful, was one which no god could forgive, so he, too was sent to Tartarus.

There were many, many others, each with his own story. Among them were the fifty daughters of Danaus, known as the Danaids. They were descendants of Io and had come from Egypt with their father when he was made king of Argos. The fifty sons of Danaus's brother, Aegyptus, had followed them, intent on marriage. Danaus appeared to agree to the mass-marriage, but in reality he was forced into it by his over-bearing brother. He let the ceremonies proceed but made the girls swear that they would stab their new husbands to death on the wedding night. All but one of the girls did as he asked and for this they were condemned to try forever to fill with water a jar riddled with holes.

These, then, were the three paths which the shade might follow. Hades himself took no part in the judges' decisions unless a serious dispute arose. In that case his word was always final. Only occasionally did Perspheone intervene – perhaps where the arguments for each side were balanced, and it was difficult to choose the right one. Persephone usually argued for the more merciful judgement, and sometimes Hades was persuaded – but no one else could sway him, nor would anyone else even dare to try.

The most important of the lesser gods in Hades was Hecate, once the moon goddess, and a daughter of Zeus. When she left the world above, she was given great authority in Hades, where she was known as the invincible queen. If the judges thought one of the dead should be allowed to make amends for his past misdeeds, it was Hecate who presided over the ceremony and over the purification that followed. However, not all her activities were peaceful. She was an enchantress, and could send evil spirits to earth to plague men who had done wrong. Sometimes she went there herself on nights when the moon was full. Her awesome figure, always accompanied by three enormous hounds, could often be seen haunting the crossroads and places where gravestones threw shadows across the grass.

The three furies – Tisiphone, Alecto and Megaera – also lived in Hades. They were quite hideous to look at, for they had the bodies of black dogs, bats' wings and snakes for hair. Though the Underworld was their home, their task was to judge the truth of complaints made by mortals against one another and to allot punishment to those they considered to be in the wrong. They were especially concerned with mortals who broke a sacred oath or who plotted the murder of their parents. No one found guilty could escape the lash of the whips they carried. To the guilty they sent out the Keres, or hounds of Hades – winged, red-robed monsters with long, pointed white teeth. The Keres would pursue their victims relentlessly, even from country to country and across the sea, until at length they swooped for the kill, their cruel jaws gaping. When they had finished, they would flap away like grim vultures, bearing their victims to the land of shadows.

Persephone among the dead

Demeter was a daughter of Cronus and Rhea and a sister of Zeus. To
the Greeks she was the goddess of the harvests, of corn and of all
living plants. Every year she ripened the golden grain and in late
summer the people offered thanks to her for the bounty of the earth.
She lived in the mountainous island of Sicily with her only daughter
Persephone. Persephone grew up to become one of the most beautiful
girls in the land, but although she was the daughter of a great goddess
she lived a quiet country life, sheltered from the quarrels and rivalries
of Olympus. Then, one day, without warning, their peaceful, happy
life was violently changed.

Persephone had gone out walking alone and did not return. Night
fell, but there was no sign of the girl and no message from her.
Demeter waited and waited but at last she summoned her servants.
'Search the fields and the hills and valleys,' she commanded them.
'Some terrible accident must have happened to prevent Persephone's
return. Search well and you will be rewarded.'

For days the searchers came and went, but they brought no news to
cheer grief-stricken Demeter. They ranged wider and wider over the
mountainous island of Sicily. Demeter herself joined them, lighting
torches from the fires of the volcano Etna so that she and her helpers
need not rest, even during the long, weary nights. But there was no
sign of Persephone. She had vanished without trace.

At last Demeter's quest took her across the sea to other lands, and
she forgot in her sorrows the mortals she should have served. The
corn crops failed, the plants and trees died, and the land became barren
under her neglect.

In the course of her wanderings Demeter came to Eleusis, a town
about ten miles to the north-east of Athens. She had disguised herself
as an old woman for she did not wish to be recognized and she was
welcomed, as all strangers were, by King Celeus and his wife Metaneira.
In talking to them she learned that their new-born child Demophoön
was in need of a nurse.
'I have to rest a while here, for I am very weary,' Demeter told them.
'Will you let me occupy my time as the nurse you need?' Though this
was the reason she gave to them, she was also beginning to give up
hope and perhaps she felt that caring for the baby would help to make
up for her own loss.

Celeus and Metaneira accepted the offer gladly, and for a time
Demeter seemed to be content with her new life. But though outwardly

she was calm and placid, the loss of Persephone and the years of searching had made her bitter.

Abas, the eldest son of Celeus, liked to tease her, but would sometimes go too far. One day, stung to sudden anger, Demeter forgot her role as nurse among the mortals and invoking her magical powers, she turned Abas instantly into a lizard. She watched him scuttle away out of sight into a crack in the walls of the room. Demeter's anger passed as quickly as it had begun and she was almost immediately alarmed and horrified by what she had done. She decided to make amends to Celeus and his wife, and at the same time to repay them for the kindness they

had always shown her, by casting a benevolent spell on their youngest child. Lifting the baby from his cradle, she crossed to the hearth and held him over the fire. In this way she could burn away his mortality and make him an immortal.

At that very moment Metaneira passed the door and saw what Demeter was doing. With a cry of horror, she rushed in and snatched the baby from the goddess. Without realizing it, she broke the spell before its purpose could be achieved, and the little Demophoön died as his mother clutched him in her arms.

Demeter knew that now she must reveal her true self. No one would believe an old nurse's

story, especially as Abas, too, was lost for ever. Throwing off her dark cloak, she stood before Metaneira as a goddess. Strangely enough, Demeter herself gained joy from this time of sorrow in a quite unexpected way. Another of Metaneira's sons, Triptolemus, had news of Persephone and when he found out who the old nurse really was, he hurried to tell her what he had heard.

On the day she disappeared, Persephone had been gathering flowers in the fields. A shepherd boy guarding his flock nearby had noticed her and stood watching as she moved slowly from clump to clump, picking a few flowers from each place. Suddenly, a tall man driving a golden chariot drawn by two black horses snatched up the girl and carried her off, vanishing as quickly as he had come into a great crevasse that opened at that moment in the hillside. The shepherd had not seen the man's face – he had been much too frightened – but Demeter guessed who it must have been. Her brother, Hades, Lord of the Underworld, was holding her only daughter prisoner among the dead.

Demeter was happy to learn that Persephone was still alive, but very angry at the trick which had been played on her. If Hades held Persephone, it was most likely with Zeus's knowledge and consent. Full of rage, she left Eleusis and continued her wanderings. All this time the land remained barren for Demeter refused to restore the earth to its former abundance. Flowers withered while they were still in bud, and blight and disease attacked any plant that managed to push its way through the hard, cold ground.

It seemed as if the whole of mankind would perish from lack of food, and even the gods were deprived of the sacrifices and gifts which they had come to expect. At last Zeus acted. He sent his son Hermes with a message to Hades, demanding Persephone's release. There was one condition: she could only leave if no food had passed her lips during her time in the Underworld, for anyone who has eaten the food of the dead owes allegiance to Hades, their king.

Hermes found Persephone sitting pale and sad beside Hades, staring out into the shadows. A bunch of dead, dried flowers still lay in her hands and every now and then she plucked absent-mindedly at their petals.
'I have eaten nothing since the day I was dragged from my home,' Persephone said. 'Every day they bring me food, tempting me with fruits more beautiful than any I have seen in the world above. But I know it is the food of the dead they offer me, and will taste bitter as ash. Oh Hermes, take me back to the sunlight!'

So Hermes carried Persephone back to the entrance of the Underworld, back past Cerberus, who licked her hand in farewell, back across the thick waters of the Styx to the cold fields of Sicily where Demeter was waiting for her. As Persephone stepped down from Hermes's chariot it was as if the world was born again. The harsh winter rolled away like fog, leaving the country-side green and fresh, with the young corn springing and flowers and blossoms adding all kinds of brilliant colours. Joyfully, Demeter and Persephone went home.

The happiness of their reunion was to be short-lived. In the Underworld, Hades called every shade and spirit before him, questioning and questioning until at last he found one who answered him in the right way. Ascalaphus had seen Persephone pick a pomegranate from the tree in the garden to quench her thirst, and had watched while she accidentally swallowed seven of the tiny pips. Hades was delighted and at once claimed Persephone back as his bride. Zeus agreed that the bargain must be kept. However, Demeter did not give up.
'Until my daughter is returned to me once more, the earth shall remain as barren as the driest desert,' she declared, wrapping her cloak tightly around her to shut away her divine power from the world.

An urgent discussion began among the gods and at last agreement was reached. For nine months of each year Persephone would live with her mother, but for the remaining three she must return to Hades and rule as queen of the Under-world. With this compromise Demeter had to be content, for the alternative was to be parted from her beloved daughter forever.

Demeter never came to terms with the months of separation. Every year while her daughter was away she went into mourning. The flowers withered, the trees shed their leaves and the earth grew cold and bare. Even the birds were silent. But every year, on Persephone's return, the spring came again. Flowers sprang up wherever she walked, the new leaves broke their buds and the birds flew about her head, welcoming her with their calls. Only when the crops had safely ripened and the grapes had been gathered in did Persephone leave once more for her winter among the shades.

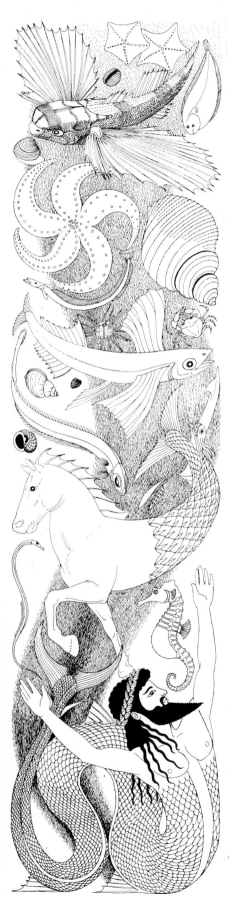

Poseidon's Ocean Kingdom

To be ruler of the seas and everything that lives in them should make even the most ambitious god contented, for there is magic and beauty in the mysterious depths not found elsewhere. As god of the sea, Poseidon could not merely enjoy his strange world, he could also harness at will the power of tempests, sending great waves to lash against the rocky shores of Greece, upsetting fishing boats and sending even the larger sailing ships flying before the wind for shelter.

When Zeus, Hades and Poseidon deposed their father Cronus, they divided the earth, the sea and the sky between them. Poseidon drew the kingdom of the oceans as his share. He was not the only god of the seas, for others had ruled there from earlier times. They seem to have been more good-natured and less jealous than the later gods, for they accepted Poseidon's domination quite happily. Oceanus, son of the Titan Uranus, was the creator of the world's waters. He took the form of a vast, endless river encircling the earth; his children were the oceans, seas, and also the lakes, rivers and small streams of the land. The sun god Helios used Oceanus to return each day to the east after driving his chariot across the sky.

Another sea god was Nereus, a kindly old man of the sea who helped sailors in distress. He is chiefly known as the father of fifty daughters, the nereids, beautiful sea nymphs who appear in many of the Greek legends as wives of both gods and men.

At first, Poseidon was content in his ocean kingdom. Off Aegae, on the coast of Euboea, some days voyage south of Athens, he built a magnificent palace on the sea bed. It was adorned with white turrets and great arched doorways encrusted with corals and shells, while on the walls of the throne room and council chambers were fine paintings of sea monsters of all kinds. In the stables was a golden chariot, drawn by white horses with golden manes and hooves. In this Poseidon would ride forth, carrying the three-pronged trident with which he had once threatened Cronus, and by which he is known.

Poseidon wished at first to marry the nereid Thetis, but he abandoned her when he learned there was a prophecy that her first-born son would grow up to be greater than his father. Such an idea was not one which a proud god like Poseidon could accept and he married instead another of Nereus's daughters, Amphitrite.

Amphitrite bore Poseidon three sons, but in spite of this, they were not happy together. Poseidon was unfaithful to his wife and treated her in a rough, unkindly way. Above all, there was his burning

ambition, which took him far from home for many months on end.

It was not long before Poseidon became discontented with his kingdom and his power over the waves. He wanted to rule the land as well, and soon turned his greedy eyes on the province of Attica, which included the great city of Athens itself. To stake his claim on it, he drove his trident into the flat, rocky top of the Acropolis, causing a spring of sea-water to gush out from the spot.

At that time the whole of Attica was under the protection of the goddess Athene, a daughter of Zeus, and therefore Poseidon's own niece. She could not allow such an invasion of her territory and to establish her own claim peacefully, she planted an olive tree beside the spring. It took root at once and was soon putting out new shoots and small, grey-green leaves. But the sea god only laughed at Athene.
'Only if you vanquish me in combat will I give up what I have claimed,' he told her. He knew, of course, that he was far stronger than Athene and that she would stand no chance in a struggle. Athene knew it too, but she agreed to fight.

However, the ever-watchful Zeus decided that he could not allow the combat to take place, and he brought the two immortals together to argue their cases before a tribunal of the gods. The gods and goddesses assembled in equal numbers to decide whether Athene or Poseidon had given Athens the more useful gift: the gods sided with Poseidon, the goddesses with Athene. Zeus, as judge, had to stand aside from the argument and was not allowed to vote: so the goddesses prevailed by one vote and Athens was restored to Athene's care.

White with anger at being thwarted, Poseidon called up the seas to flood the land where Athene lived, sending huge waves crashing over the buildings of her own city, destroying her temple and the houses, farms and villages of her people. From that time, Athene went to live in Athens, taking it into her special protection.

Even after he had destroyed her home, Poseidon did not forgive Athene, nor was his ambition in any way curbed. He next tried to seize the city of Troezen from her, but Zeus once more intervened and ruled that they must share the produce of the city. Unsatisfied, Poseidon tried unsuccessfully to take the island of Aegina from Zeus himself, and the island of Naxos from Zeus's son Dionysus. Finally, he laid claim to some land which

belonged to Hera. This time Zeus could not make Poseidon even begin to see reason.
'It has been proved time and again that the gods are against me,' Poseidon argued when his brother suggested that the gods should once more sit in judgement to decide his claim.
'The river gods are fair men,' said Zeus after a while. 'Will you stand by what *they* say?'

Poseidon shrugged his massive shoulders. 'I suppose we can try,' he said grudgingly. He hoped that they would not dare to go against one who commanded waters so much more mighty than theirs. However, Inachus, Asterion and Cephissus, the three river gods, were not afraid to give judgement in Hera's favour. Once more Poseidon flew into a towering rage.

This time, instead of flooding the land, he caused the rivers in which the gods lived to dry up, turning them into dusty, stony pathways and stranding the gods and river nymphs on the withered banks. Only when the winter rains came did the rivers flow again, and every summer since that time, they shrink and dwindle away.

All the animals of the ocean owed allegiance to Poseidon, from the great whales to the smallest coral fish. There were also less familiar creatures. The nereids could sometimes be seen playing in the waves around their grotto home with strange beings called Tritons. These had scaly bodies and fins, and were half man, half fish. They took their name from Poseidon's son Triton, who was himself half a man and half a fish. Though they played gently enough with the nereids, they could be fierce creatures and had sharp teeth and hands with great hooked claws. Sometimes they left the sea to invade the land, spreading terror wherever they went.

Proteus, son of Oceanus, was Poseidon's herdsman and guardian of his seals. Each day they would sleep around him on a wide, flat-topped rock while the midday sun shone down and waves lapped lazily at the shore. It was at this time that those who wished to know what the future held came to consult him, for he had the gift of prophecy. Before Proteus would speak, however, the questioner had to catch him, for Proteus had a thousand forms, and would turn himself into anything he liked when a stranger appeared. It might be a dragon or a lion, or any fabulous beast. Only if the stranger showed he was not afraid, would Proteus become himself again and look into the strange world of the future.

Prometheus and Pandora

According to the early Greeks, Zeus and Prometheus were the makers of man. Prometheus was a Titan, one of the old gods who had supported Zeus in his struggle against Cronus. It was Prometheus who fashioned the first men out of clay, shaping them to walk upright, looking towards the gods. Zeus gave them the breath of life.

These first men and women were still primitive beings, living on what they could kill with their wooden bows, horn axes, and knives, and on the few crops they knew how to grow. They had no knowledge of fire, so their food was eaten raw, and they wrapped themselves in thick furs to keep out the cold of winter. They could not make bowls or jars in which to store things, for without ovens they could not harden the clay; nor could they work metals to make efficient tools and weapons.

Zeus was happy that they should remain like this, for he was afraid that otherwise some of them might one day grow to rival him in power. The more thoughtful Prometheus had learned to love mankind. He knew that with his help, they could progress beyond their primitive state: it was the human race he and Zeus had set out to create, not just another animal.

'They must be taught the secret of making fire,' he told Zeus, 'otherwise they are as helpless as children. We must finish what we have begun.'

But Zeus was firm. 'They are content with what they have,' he answered. 'They know no better, so why should we concern ourselves?'

Prometheus realized that he could never persuade Zeus to agree with him, so he went secretly to Olympus, where fires burned both day and night, and lit a torch. With this he heated a piece of charcoal until it glowed red. He hid the burning charcoal in the hollow, ribbed stalk of a herb called fennel that grew nearby on the mountainside and, blowing out the torch, he crept away unseen with the stalk of fennel under his cloak.

From the first earthly fire, lighted from this charcoal, men made many more, and Prometheus taught them how to use it to its best advantage. He helped them in other ways, too. For example, when sacrifices were made, the choicest pieces of meat were always set aside for the gods. The less nourishing parts which remained were given to man. By a trick, Prometheus made sure that man obtained his proper share. He divided the meat of an ox into two equal-sized parcels. One, however, contained only bones and fat, wrapped in a section of hide.

The other contained the better meat. Zeus, deceived at first, stored up his wrath in silence.

With Prometheus's help, man developed rapidly. He learned to fashion pots and vases, fine ornaments for decorating himself, buildings made from hard-baked clay blocks, with roofs that were tiled instead of being thatched with reeds. He learned the art of metalwork so that he could defend himself and go hunting with a sword and spear. But Zeus, watching from the skies one night, saw a fire burning on earth and knew that he had been tricked. He sent for Prometheus.
'Did I not forbid you to show man the secret of fire?' he asked. 'They say you are wise, but can you not see that with help like yours, man will one day challenge even the gods?'
'If he is loved and taught as he should be, that will not happen,' Prometheus replied.

But Zeus was angry and would not see reason. He ordered Prometheus to be seized and had him taken far away to the mountains of the east, where he was chained to a rock. A fierce eagle fed daily on his liver and each morning the liver grew again so that the torture could begin once more. It was many years before Prometheus was released – some say thirty thousand – and it is not certain how this came about. According to one legend it was the mighty Hercules who rescued him. Zeus, however, was not content to avenge himself only on his fellow god. Mankind, too, must suffer for Prometheus's goodness to them.

Zeus commanded his crippled son Hephaestus to model a girl from clay. He made Athene breathe life into her and instruct her in the womanly arts of fine sewing and cooking; Hermes the quick-witted taught her guile, deception and a false charm, and Aphrodite showed her how to be desirable to all men. Other goddesses robed her in a dress of silver and placed a garland of flowers on her hair. The girl was brought before Zeus.
'Take this casket,' he said, passing her a box of burnished copper. 'It is yours, but though you must always keep it by you, you must never in any circumstances open it. Do not ask me why, but be happy that the gods should have given you all that any woman could desire.'

Pandora, for that was the name which the girl had been given, smiled to herself. She thought that Zeus meant that the box was full of jewels and precious stones.
'Now we must find a husband who will love you as you should be loved,' Zeus went on, 'and I know just the man. Epimetheus is handsome and

young and will give you a good life down on earth.'

Epimetheus was the brother of Prometheus, an irresponsible young man who lacked his brother's wisdom. Prometheus had long ago warned him never to put great trust in or to accept gifts from Zeus, but he was flattered and perhaps a little afraid to refuse when Zeus offered him Pandora as a wife. Hermes was chosen to escort Pandora to her new husband in the world of men.
'Behold, good Epimetheus,' he said. 'Is Pandora not the most beautiful woman you have ever seen? She comes bearing a casket as her dowry. See she guards it carefully, for it must never be opened. Who can tell what might happen if she looked inside.'

Epimetheus took the box from Pandora and locked it safely away. At first Pandora was so happy with her new life that she forgot about the box, but as time went on she wondered about it more and more often. She tried to find the key to the cupboard where her husband had placed it for safety, but he carried it always on his belt.
'Why can't we have just one small glimpse inside?' she would ask him, day after day.

One day, when Epimetheus was sleeping soundly, Pandora crept into his room and took the key. She put the casket on a table and turned the key in the lock. For a moment she hesitated, fear overcoming her curiosity. It was only for a moment, however, and then she lifted the lid.

As she did so there was the rushing sound of a great wind, and Pandora stepped back. Out of the box flew all the evils which have troubled us ever since that moment – hardship, poverty, old age, sickness, jealousy, vice, passion and distrust. Desperately Pandora tried to close the lid, but it was too late. The box's contents were scattered far and wide in the world. Zeus's revenge was now almost complete. The men Prometheus had fashioned with such skill and taught so patiently could no longer be the noble race he had intended. Instead, their life was to be a constant struggle against all kinds of hardships. There seemed little chance of man now reaching out for Zeus's throne.

But Zeus had not triumphed altogether. Fearfully, Pandora approached the casket and looked inside. One thing remained at the very bottom and as she slammed the lid down and turned the key she trapped it. It was hope. By saving this, mankind had found a way of surviving in his new, hostile world: with hope he had a reason for going on living.

Aphrodite, goddess of love

There was great excitement in the court of Zeus, for his wife Hera was about to bear him another child. Zeus had predicted that it would be a son and had already chosen the name Hephaestus for the baby. Physicians bustled about with an air of importance and the gods spoke in whispers so as not to disturb Hera.

The birth was long and difficult and when the boy was born, he was deformed and ugly. The nurses who attended Hera tried for as long as possible to keep the baby away from her, for they knew that she had set her heart on bearing a young god who would grow to outshine all others in his looks, fine bearing and strength. Of course Hera demanded to see her child and when she saw how stunted and weak he was, she flew into a rage.

'This is no child of mine!' she stormed. Rising from her bed, she seized Hephaestus by one of his short, twisted legs and before any of the horrified watchers could stop her, hurled him from Olympus.

Down, down, down he fell, through the clouds, past rocky cliffs towards the earth. By good fortune an arm of the sea stretched inland where he fell, and two nereids, Thetis and Eurynome, were waiting to catch him in their arms as he sank under the waves. They cared for him well, taking pity on his ugliness and treating him as if he were their own child, so that he grew up happily in the underwater world.

Years passed, and Hephaestus became a young man of great talent. Though his legs remained weak and crooked, his arms were strong and he became skilled in the art of decorative work in iron and other metals. Thetis prepared a blacksmith's forge and workshop in a grotto deep under the sea. Here he worked, making all kinds of metal objects. In spite of the apparent clumsiness of his misshapen hands, he was a gifted designer and could fashion the most delicate jewellery.

Thetis and Eurynome loved to wear the necklaces and bracelets that Hephaestus made, and felt that they had been well repaid for their care of the strange, stunted god who had fallen from the sky. Hephaestus, too, was contented to do the work he loved and it seemed that their peaceful existence would go on for ever.

One day Thetis dressed herself in her finest robes and placed a pendant which Hephaestus had made for her round her neck. The centre of the pendant was a pearl almost as large as a pigeon's egg, surrounded by blue jewels gathered from the sea bed and mounted in silver tracery. The pearl shone like the moon and Thetis was pleased, for she had been invited to a festival of the gods and knew that her lovely pendant would be the envy of them all.

She was right. Hera at once singled her out and asked who the craftsman might be who had made such a fabulous thing. Thetis knew how badly Hera had treated her baby son and that Hephaestus wished to have nothing further to do with her, but she was caught off her guard. 'I – I have forgotten his name,' she stammered. 'If you will be patient it may come back to me.' 'Nonsense,' exclaimed Hera, who had seen Thetis's hesitation and her blushes. The nereid was not used to telling lies. 'You must at least know where he lives and works, even if you cannot remember what he is called – which I very much doubt.'

Poor Thetis tried hard not to tell, but she was no match for Hera. At last she had to confess that the jeweller was none other than Hera's own despised son.

'Then send him to me at once,' commanded Hera. 'I will try,' said Thetis doubtfully. 'But he is a man now, and goes his own way.'

As Thetis had suspected, Hephaestus refused to leave his home in the sea. He had neither forgotten nor forgiven Hera for her unmotherly behaviour. Instead, he set to work at once to make her a present, a beautifully ornamented golden chair. Hera accepted it as a peace offering, convinced that soon he would come to her himself.

Hera seated herself proudly on her new throne, admiring the exquisite workmanship, boasting to her ladies-in-waiting about her brilliant son. It was not until she tried to get up again that it became clear the beautiful golden chair was not quite what it seemed. Though she twisted and struggled, Hera could not move. The Queen of Olympus, wife of Zeus, was held as if in a vice, beating her hands helplessly against the carved armrests. Baffled and angry she called on Zeus to help her, but even he could do nothing. His spells and incantations were useless. Hera grew desperate. 'Hephaestus must be *made* to come and release me,' she ordered. 'I will not be humbled like this by my own son.' As well as being angry, she knew that she must present a ridiculous figure sitting there in her golden chair, unable to move. She sensed that the other gods were laughing at her behind her back.

Zeus sent first messengers and then some of the gods themselves to plead with Hephaestus, but the smith god stood firm. Finally Hephaestus's own brother, Dionysus, succeeded in making him so fuddled with wine that he gave way and left his home deep in the sea to return to Olympus.

Once there he decided that Hera had suffered enough and released her from the chair. In return, she had a magnificent workshop and forge built for him, carved out of the side of a mountain. It was said that the workshop had no less than twenty bellows and twenty anvils. All the helpers Hephaestus needed were provided so that he could exceed by far the wonderful things he had already produced. Ornaments, weapons, decorative furniture, Hephaestus made them all. He was so inventive that he even created mechanical women who could do any task he set them. He now had everything he wanted except one thing – a wife. As a final gesture of reconciliation Hera promised him the hand of Aphrodite, the matchless goddess of love.

Even before the wedding took place, Hephaestus was in trouble again. He was naturally delighted with the idea of marrying Aphrodite, especially as he knew that he was too ugly to win the most beautiful woman in the world without Hera's help. In his gratitude he was unwise enough to side with his mother in one of her frequent quarrels with Zeus. Zeus was so angry with him that he hurled him once more from the heights of Olympus. This time there were no sea nymphs to break his fall, no cool, deep water to save him. He landed on the rocky slopes of a hill on the island of Lemnos, breaking both his crooked legs in a dozen places. Now more crippled than ever, he had to make golden braces for his legs so that he could stand upright and walk to meet his bride – but Zeus at least forgave him.

To the ancient Greeks, Aphrodite was the symbol of all that was beautiful and desirable – the goddess of love itself. The strange story of her origin goes back to the Age of the Titans, when Cronus fought and killed his father Uranus with a scythe. Uranus's dismembered body was thrown down into the sea and, around it the waves boiled into a pure white column of foam. From the very centre of this, like the most exquisite of sea nymphs, rose Aphrodite, outshining even the sun with her beauty.

Poseidon the sea god carried her in his chariot to Cythera, an island off the Laconian coast. Poseidon hoped to keep Aphrodite for himself, but news of her strange birth reached Zeus and he had her brought to Olympus.

Aphrodite stood in the council chamber, not at all abashed by the admiring looks of the gods assembled to welcome her. Admiration from either

gods or mortals was like the sweetest wine to her and only seemed to increase her beauty. Though her loveliness on its own would have been enough to fascinate everyone who saw her, she wore round her waist a magic girdle with the power to make all men love her. Certainly all the gods had already fallen under her spell, and one by one they demonstrated their special powers in an attempt to impress her.

Poseidon felt that he had the strongest claim of them all, for it was he who had found her. 'You came from the sea, and the sea is my kingdom, so you are mine,' he thundered. 'Everything that lies beneath the waves shall be yours, and you shall live in a grotto shining with pearls.' Raising his trident high, he caused a tempest which lashed the sea into a fury, to show his domination over it. A great tidal wave crashed into the bays and inlets, tossing fishermen like toys and tearing great rocks from the cliffs.

Hermes promised to take Aphrodite round the world in a golden chariot so that she could see faraway places and learn many things. 'The burning heart of the desert lands, the wild beasts of the jungles, the icy beauty of the wastelands of the north, fine people with skins as black as ebony – all these you shall see with me,' he promised.

Apollo also tried to convince her that he was the one she should choose, singing her a special song of love. But Aphrodite remained silent. She smiled to herself, knowing that with the help of her magic girdle she could win any – or all – of them as and when she pleased. She need not decide now. There was plenty of time and, if she was patient, something even better might come along – a god more handsome and more powerful

even than those who stood so eagerly before her.

In fact she did not have the opportunity of choosing – or of waiting – for Hera was determined that Aphrodite should be the bride of Hephaestus. 'And the sooner the better,' she thought to herself, for she had seen how Zeus's eyes shone with longing as he looked at the young goddess. 'Come forward, Hephaestus,' she commanded and the other gods, wondering, made way for him as he came limping from the back of the hall. 'Take Aphrodite for your wife, for she is yours by my decree.'

Hephaestus was, of course, overjoyed but everyone else was watching Aphrodite's face as she saw for the first time the poor cripple who was to be her husband. A god he certainly was, but a god with arms more like a gorilla's than a man's, with legs that would not support him without braces and a head as big as a giant's. Surely, they thought, she will recoil in horror or fly into a rage for quite apart from his twisted body, what could Hephaestus offer her to compare with the gifts of the other gods? The heat and dust of the forge after the cool clean water of Poseidon's kingdom; the sound of hammers after the strings of Apollo's lute?

But Aphrodite just smiled as calmly as before, and embraced Hephaestus. She guessed at once that he was a man who would not try to rule her as the others would have done. Married to him, she could do as she pleased, which was just what she wanted. Not knowing what was passing through her mind, Hera and the other gods decided that perhaps the choice had, after all, been a wise one. Poseidon, Hermes and Apollo were puzzled and a little resentful but they withdrew and went about their own business without arguing. The matter was settled.

As might have been expected, marriage to the goddess of love was not easy. Soon it was plain that she preferred the company of other men to that of her husband, and word eventually reached Hephaestus that she was spending most of her time with the hot-headed Ares. He determined to find out if the rumour was true or not and, if possible, to catch them together.

Hephaestus made a net from bronze wire, wire so fine that it was almost invisible, but worked and twisted so that it was stronger than a thousand cords. When it was finished he told Aphrodite that he would be away for a few days. Then, stealing secretly into Ares's house, he hung the net among the draperies over the war god's bed, hiding it carefully among the heavy folds. Waving goodbye to Aphrodite he set off as if on a long journey, but after a mile or two he turned back and slipped unnoticed into the war god's bedroom.

That night Aphrodite made her way to Ares's house, hardly caring whether anyone saw her or not. Hephaestus's scheme worked just as he had planned. Hidden in the bedroom, he waited until the pair were together on the bed, then pulled a bronze wire which dropped the net right over them. Though they struggled and tore at the wire, they were soon so enmeshed that there was no chance of escape.

There they lay, trapped like two helpless birds. The other gods soon found out what had happened, and at first found it all very amusing. Many of them called to mock the prisoners. The goddesses, however, were shocked at Aphrodite's behaviour – as well as being rather jealous of her. 'It's a fair punishment for a wanton wife,' said one. 'What else could he do?'
'I knew something like this would happen the moment I saw her,' said another. 'Women like that cannot be trusted.'
'A wife should behave like a wife,' said another 'even Hephaestus is not all bad.'

Eventually, however, Hephaestus was persuaded to release them – but not before Ares had paid compensation. Gold coins, precious swords and shields, the spoils of a hundred battles were gathered together to be stored deep in the mountainside for all time.

Ridicule had been an apt punishment for Ares. Though he raged and shouted, swaggering about as if nothing had happened, he knew he had been made to look thoroughly foolish and took care to do nothing more to offend Hephaestus. Aphrodite, however, seemed quite unashamed. She was the goddess of love, after all, and it was not in her nature to behave cautiously for very long. The temptation to use the magic girdle to bend men to her will was too strong, and many times Hephaestus had good cause to regret that he had married her.

Time passed and still Aphrodite did not change. Whenever there was a celebration she was always an important visitor and of course at any wedding she was guest of honour. One day she attended the wedding of Thetis, one of the nereids who had cared for Hephaestus as a child. Thetis was marrying a mortal, King Peleus of Phthia. It was a happy occasion of the kind Aphrodite loved, with dancing to the music of pipes and flutes. The banqueting table glowed with the bright colours of flowers and the gleaming gold and silver bowls were piled high with food.

In the middle of the feasting, Eris, one of the guests, threw down a golden apple on to the floor. Cut in the apple's golden skin were the words 'To the most beautiful woman of all'. It lay there for a moment, then three of the goddesses together reached out to claim it: Hera, Athene and, of course, Aphrodite. No one wanted to decide between them but eventually Paris, the young son of the king of Troy was chosen as the judge.

Paris was a handsome, confident young man and was not at all afraid of the three jealous goddesses. He made them stand in a circle around him, walking slowly from one to the other as he considered their claims: Hera, Queen of Heaven, Athene who was wise as well as beautiful – and Aphrodite, gay and laughing, looking at him with mocking eyes as if his decision was the most obvious thing in the world. Smiling back at her, Paris handed her the golden apple.

This small incident was to have consequences that even wise Athene could not guess at. Shortly after, Paris fell deeply in love with Helen, a daughter of Zeus who was married to a Greek king called Menelaus. With Aphrodite's grateful help, he succeeded in kidnapping Helen and carrying her off to his home in Troy. The story of the long war which followed as the Greeks fought to recapture Helen is told later in the book. Aphrodite, temptress and enchantress, may have played only a small part in this, but it is one which is typical of her life. She seemed fated to set men against one another.

Ares, god of war

Fierce quarrels were not rare among the Greek heroes, both between gods and among the mortals, but even the immortals found the behaviour of Ares and his family rather more than they could accept. When the others fought, they liked to think that they had good reason to do so, for freedom, or to right a wrong – though to be truthful this was not always borne out by the facts. However, Ares seemed to like fighting for its own sake, and would rush headlong into any battle, regardless of the rights and wrongs of the cause. Unfortunately for him he was often far from successful.

In view of his record, it is surprising that he was the Greek god of war, particularly as other gods, especially Athene, were far better at fighting than he was. Probably it was his enthusiasm and hot temper which made men seek his support for their quarrels, secure in the knowledge that he would not bother too much about the justice of the cause. His sister, Eris, was just as short-tempered as he was, and her jealous plotting often caused wars between cities or states. This was just what Ares thrived on. They would be joined in the fighting by his two sons, with the savage, man-eating horses he had given them to pull their war chariots. Altogether, they formed a formidable family.

The only one among the gods who delighted in Ares's deeds was Hades, for frequent wars meant that his underworld kingdom received a constant stream of young warriors slain on the field of battle. Amongst the goddesses, Aphrodite alone was prepared to put up with his impetuous temperament but, as we have seen, the great war god gained little honour from their friendship.

In his time, the war god fought twice in battles against armies commanded by the much more skilful Athene. He lost both. During the great war of Troy, he also clashed with Athene. In this war, the gods took definite sides, often fighting to support their chosen heroes, and sometimes rescuing them if they seemed to be losing the battle. Athene supported the Greek side, Ares was for the Trojans. During a day of particularly fierce fighting, Ares was attacked by the Greek hero Diomedes. Usually, a god would have been able to win such a contest easily, but Diomedes had immortal help himself. Athene, hidden under a helmet of darkness, took over his war chariot. When Diomedes seemed to be tiring, she charged at Ares, firing arrows from her silver bow. Badly wounded, Ares fled groaning back to Olympus.

Ares was also involved in a battle among the gods themselves. Two sons of Poseidon, Otus and Ephialtes, plotted to climb up to Mount

Olympus and take the home of the gods by force. Once there, they planned to carry off Hera and Artemis.

Ephialtes and Otus were giants of men, nine fathoms tall, and of enormous strength. Their plan was in keeping with their size: it was no less than to pile two mountains, Pelion and Ossa, on top of one another so that by using them as huge stepping stones, they could reach the heights of Olympus itself.

Such a massive undertaking could scarcely go unnoticed, and Zeus soon heard of the preparations which were being made to move the rocky, pine-covered mountains. He called his armies together immediately and made ready to fight the invaders. Ares, of course, rushed to join the battle. For once he was on the right side, but though Zeus defeated the two giants utterly, before he had done so, Ares had been taken prisoner. He vanished completely.

Though a long and thorough search was made, it is hardly surprising that he was not found, for the beaten giants had hidden him in a bronze jar, from which it was impossible to escape. For thirteen months he was imprisoned there, a seemingly endless time, during which he grew weak and thin, and very cramped indeed.

The search had long been abandoned when one day Hermes happened to pass on his travels the barn where the jar was stored. It was growing dark and Hermes was weary. The barn looked inviting and warm, and he settled down to sleep on a pile of hay in one corner.

He was just drifting into sleep when he heard a faint tapping sound. At first he took no notice of it, for he imagined that it was simply the noise of rats feeding on the sacks of grain in the loft above him. But the tapping persisted and at length, unable to go to sleep again, he got up to investigate. In the gloom of one corner of the barn he found a tall jar, and the sound seemed to come from this.

'Perhaps a rat has fallen in and cannot get out,' he said to himself, and he pulled the jar across the earth floor to where the moon shed its light through the open doorway. He tapped lightly on the jar, and, to his surprise, heard frantic knocking in reply. Feeling slightly foolish, he addressed the jar:

'Who's in there? You are making a lot of noise for a rat!'

'It is I, Ares,' came a faint reply. 'Let me out of this prison and you shall have anything a mighty god can grant.'

'Ares! However did you get into that humiliating position. But don't despair, I will set you free.'

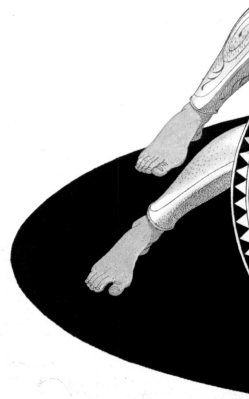

In a moment, Hermes had unsealed the jar and lifted its heavy lid. Stretching and groaning, a thin and dusty Ares, his armour tarnished and his beard curling around his twisted limbs, dragged himself out into the moonlight.

And so, at long last, Ares was freed to fight another day – and, knowing his nature, we can be sure he did so.

42

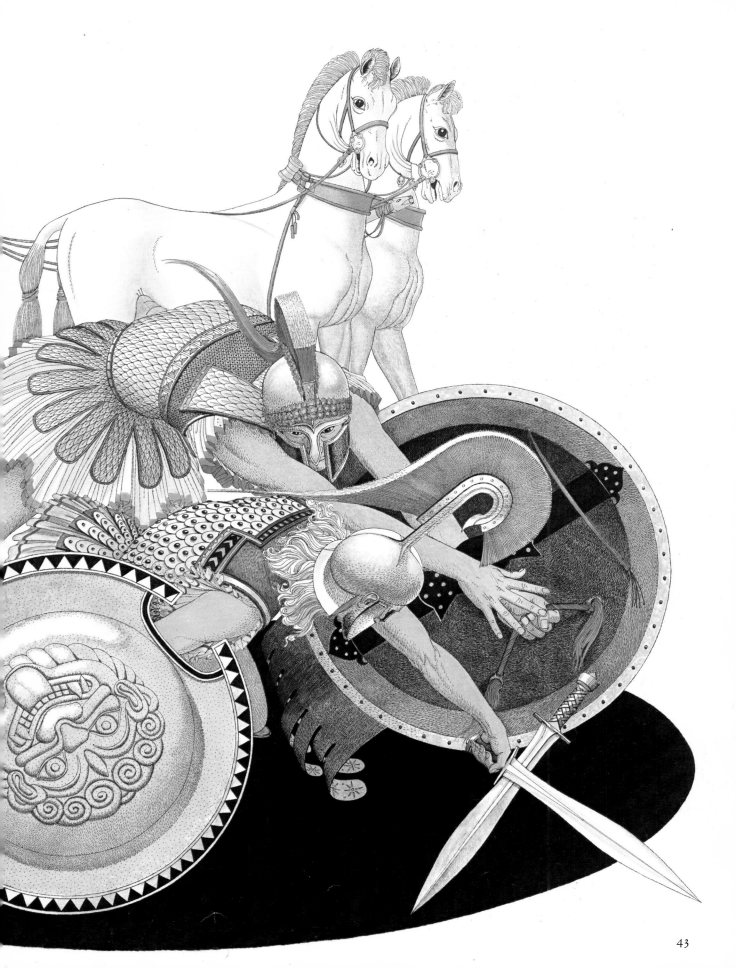

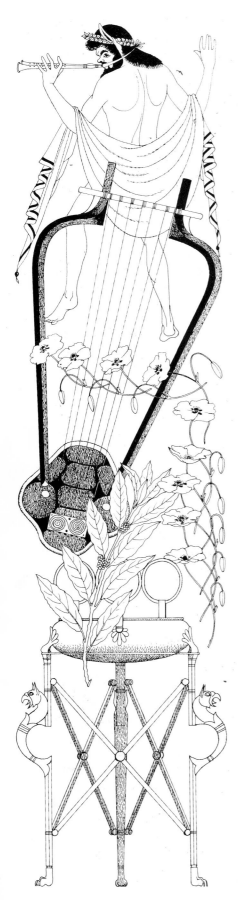

Artemis and Apollo

Among the gods of Olympus, marriage was not thought of as the lifelong union of one man and one woman, with no one coming between them. If the gods had thought as we do, there would be far less to tell about them, and their myths and legends would be far less entertaining than they are. Regrettable as it may be, a peaceful and virtuous life does not produce spell-binding stories. This may be why Hestia, goddess of the hearth and symbol of the home and family, does not feature very largely in the Greek myths. Though she was of considerable importance to the ancient Greeks, and a hearth was consecrated to her in every home, Hestia slew no monsters; nor did she have romantic adventures with the gods and mortals.

It was probably Zeus who set the worst example of all: there seems to be no end to the stories of beautiful girls he pursued. One of these was Leto, a daughter of the Titans, who lived in Olympus. When Hera learned that Leto was to bear Zeus a child, she banished her, sending the serpent Python to pursue her wherever she went, so that she could get no rest.

After nine weary months Leto reached Ortygia on the coast of Sicily, and there she gave birth to a daughter, Artemis. Still haunted by Python, she crossed immediately to the island of Delos in the Aegean Sea. Here, where Python could not follow her, Artemis's twin brother Apollo was born. Both Artemis and Apollo were fine children and, like their mother, were very beautiful to look at. On their third birthday, Zeus visited them and he was so proud of what he saw that he decided they must be brought to Olympus.

The years passed and Zeus sent for the twins.
'See, Apollo,' he said, 'I have a gift for you.' And he took the youth outside to show him a golden chariot with white horses harnessed to it. They were fine animals with great, arched necks and flowing manes, and they moved restlessly between the shafts of the chariot, impatient to race away across the sky with their new master. In the chariot lay a golden bow and a quiver of golden arrows.
'All these Hephaestus has made for you, using his finest materials and subtlest skills,' Zeus told his son. Then he turned to Artemis. 'I was less sure what would please you,' he said, 'and so I have left you to choose what you would like. Tell me and it shall be yours.'

Artemis did not hesitate. In many ways she was like her twin brother, and her tastes, too, were for a life of action in the open air. A home and family held no appeal for her, and both she and Apollo, as they grew up, had been happiest roaming the lonely mountainsides that surrounded their home, hunting the deer which lived there.

'Give me a bow and arrows, and a chariot like Apollo's,' she said. 'But make mine of silver, not of gold, and give me also a hunting tunic of silver thread which I may wear for the chase. And I would like a pack of fierce, fleet-footed hounds and twenty wood nymphs and twenty water nymphs to be my handmaidens and companions.'

Unlike most girls of her age, Artemis thought nothing of men, and had resolved to remain a virgin. In spite of this, the Greeks worshipped her as the protectress of little children – because, it is said, her mother had borne her without pain.

The one-eyed giants, the Cyclopes, who forged the thunderbolts for Zeus, made Artemis her silver bow and arrows, guided as usual by Hephaestus. The god Pan provided hounds bred in Sparta and Artemis herself picked out the fairest nymphs from the woods and the streams. When all her gifts were assembled, Artemis sent two of the swiftest hounds out into the hills. 'Run fast, run free,' she commanded them, 'and bring me back two fine deer. But see that they are not harmed. Do not delay, for I have waited many days to try my skill with my father's gifts.'

The hounds returned with their quarry, two hinds with spreading antlers, and Artemis harnessed these to her chariot. Then, cracking her whip above their heads, she gave a wild cry and dashed away into the hills, exulting in her new found freedom. Behind her, like the swiftest of fawns, ran her nymphs, and the hounds streamed out before her, their deep baying echoing from the rocks around.

Night fell before Artemis had found a worthy target for her silver arrows, so she lit a torch from the fires of Mount Olympus and by its light took aim at a tall pine tree, splitting it quite in half with her speeding arrow. Next morning, another of her arrows pierced a wild boar, which fell dead instantly. Artemis had not yet found a target to match her skill and she roamed on, searching by day and sleeping at night under the shelter of the trees. At last she came to an evil city where injustice ruled, and all the inhabitants lived wicked, selfish lives. As she passed, she fired her third arrow into the centre of the town. Scattering into thousands of shining, deadly pieces, the single arrow killed the whole population in the same instant.

News of this and tales of her skill spread about the country, and Artemis soon became known as the goddess of the chase, as the huntress, and as goddess of the moon, by whose silvery light she so often hunted.

Artemis kept strictly to her vow not to become involved with men. When the river god Alpheius fell in love with her and followed her, she made her nymphs daub their faces with clay from the river bank. She did the same, and together they mocked Alpheius, who could no longer tell one from another and had to abandon his pursuit. The nymphs, too, had made a vow of chastity, but some of them were not as strong-willed as Artemis herself, particularly when Zeus was around. Few women could resist him, and one of the nymphs, Callisto, was soon persuaded to abandon her vows.

Artemis was angry when she learned that Callisto was to bear Zeus's child. Her rage at this betrayal of her way of life was so great that she changed Callisto into a bear, intending to hunt it down with her hounds, and tear it to pieces. Fortunately, Zeus acted more swiftly. He snatched the bear up to heaven before the hounds could track it down, setting it among the stars – where it can still be seen today.

The youth Actaeon was not so lucky. He once came upon Artemis bathing naked in a stream. Enchanted with her beauty, he stayed to watch her and indignantly, Artemis turned him into a stag. His own hounds hunted him to death.

While Artemis was running through the wild hills and woods of Greece, Apollo, too, was learning to use the gifts of Zeus. He had never forgotten the tales which his mother Leto had told of the evil serpent Python. He now discovered that Python had its lair in a cave on the side of Mount Parnassus. Driving there swiftly and silently in his chariot, he surprised Python sleeping in the sunshine outside its cave. Apollo took aim and sent a golden arrow speeding on its way. The great coils of the serpent's body writhed as the arrow struck, and it hissed its hatred into the mountain air. However, it was only wounded, not killed, and it slid away among the rocks.

Python fled to the sacred shrine of Delphi and took refuge there, but again Apollo hunted it down. This time he did not trust to a single arrow, but let fly again and again until Python lay dead at his feet in the sacred grove.

Delphi, nestling in wooded mountains, was the place where the oracles of Mother Earth were pronounced. Even the gods consulted the oracle here, and they were outraged that murder had been committed in such a holy place. They demanded that Apollo do penance for his deed. Instead, Apollo claimed Delphi for his own, seized the Delphic oracle and instituted annual games, to be played on a great arena high on the hillside above the temple. They were named the Pythian Games in honour of his victory over Python.

Apollo was a fine musician, renowned for the sweetness of his music and the gentle touch of his fingers on the strings of his lyre. No one had ever been known to surpass him, but soon after he had claimed Delphi, he began to hear people praising a satyr, Marsyas, whose flute playing was said to be superior to any of Apollo's music. Marsyas, being simple by nature, did not have the sense to deny this, and Apollo jealously summoned him.

'The Muses will judge which of us is the finer player,' declared Apollo. 'And whoever wins can do what he likes with the loser.'

Marsyas was too frightened to disagree with a god, so the contest was arranged. First one played his sweetest music, then the other, each trying to outplay the other. The Muses consulted together, shaking their heads wisely, but for all their wisdom, they could not decide who was the best. Apollo was annoyed.

'We will try a further test,' he said. 'We will turn our instruments upside down and play again. As I am a god and you are only a lowly satyr, I claim precedence: I will play first,' he added haughtily.

So Apollo turned his lyre upside down and sang sweetly to the music as he played, sounding this time even better than before. When he had finished, poor Marsyas lifted his flute to his lips and instantly realized that he had been tricked, for it is quite impossible to play a flute upside down, and equally useless to try to sing while you are playing.

Marsyas payed a high price for his simplicity, for Apollo's cruel revenge was to flay him alive and to nail his skin to a pine tree beside the river which flowed nearby. To this day, the river bears the unlucky satyr's name.

Those who accepted a challenge from the gods did so at their peril, but it was sad that Apollo chose to use a trick to win his contest; even if it

had progressed fairly, he must in the end have been judged the winner, for he was the god of music itself, and the sweet sounds of his lyre filled the air at the banquets of the immortals.

Apollo, like most of the other gods, could turn himself into other forms to get what he wanted. One day the nymph Dryope was guarding her father's flocks with her friends the dryads, the nymphs of the trees. As the sheep grazed the short grass, she gathered wild white cystus flowers, which grow on the lower slopes of the mountains of Greece. Apollo, who was wandering near, saw the group of nymphs, but thought that he might frighten them if he came on them too suddenly. Even from a distance, Dryope's beauty was dazzling, and the last thing he wanted was for her to run away from him in terror.

Without a sound, Apollo turned himself into a tortoise and in this disguise ambled slowly towards the little group. The girls were delighted with this distraction. One by one they held the tortoise, passing him from hand to hand, intrigued by the yellow and black pattern on its shell. When Dryope reached for it, she claimed it as her own and put it inside her tunic, exactly as Apollo had planned. Instantly he turned himself into a snake and, rearing his head from

the folds of Dryope's dress, he hissed fiercely at the other nymphs. Terrified, they took flight, while Dryope fell fainting to the ground. When she awoke, Apollo's strong arms were around her, his lips on hers.

Apollo was soon found with another girl, a princess of Thessaly called Coronis. Coronis was in love with a young prince called Ischys. However, she accepted Apollo as her lover, and bore him a child.

Apollo suspected that Coronis did not love him as much as she loved Ischys and when he had to go on a journey shortly after the child was born, he left a white crow behind to spy on her. He had only been gone a few days when the crow came winging across the mountains to tell him that at that very moment Coronis was with her mortal love.

'False bird!' raged Apollo, venting his anger most unfairly on the crow. 'Why did you not watch her more closely and come to me sooner? You must pay the price for your neglect. From this day you, and all that come after you, shall be black as the darkest night!'

As he spoke, the crow's feathers turned from white to dull black – and to this day, all the crow family bear the mark of his curse.

Apollo wished also to punish Coronis, though he could not face harming her himself. Instead he called on Artemis, and she shot the girl dead with a single arrow from her silver bow.

Coronis's child, Asclepius, was saved and under the expert teaching of Chiron the centaur he grew up to be a skilled surgeon. It was said that he brought men from the very gates of the Underworld, restoring them to health when everyone had given them up as lost. Hades complained to Zeus that he was being robbed of his rightful subjects and, to appease the Lord of the Underworld, Zeus struck Asclepius dead.

Now it was Apollo's turn to fly into a fury. In his anger he cared nothing for the power of Zeus and bore down in his golden chariot on the forge of the Cyclopes, makers of the thunderbolt, slaying them all with the bow they had themselves made for him. It was only through the pleading of Leto that Apollo was saved from eternal banishment to Tartarus. As it was, he spent one long, dark year among the damned, far from the open hills and sky that he loved, far, far from the sound of music. During the year Apollo seemed to gain a patience and wisdom that he had not possessed before. Thereafter, his life was one of great peace and tranquillity.

The chariot of the sun

Helios, son of the Titans Hyperion and Thea, was the god who drove the chariot of the sun each day from east to west across the sky, spreading light and warmth over the world. At nightfall, he would return to his home in the east in a great golden bowl, borne on the river Oceanus, which encircled the earth. There he would rest before preparing to set off once more on his journey as morning drew near again.

His chariot was of gold, drawn by four fiery horses with golden manes, and he himself wore a golden helmet, sparkling with jewels of all kinds. Everyone who looked at him had to shade their eyes to avoid being blinded by the dazzling shafts of light that played all around him.

Phaethon was Helios's son by Clyme the nereid, one of the fifty daughters of Nereus the sea god. He was brought up in the then fertile land of Egypt. Though Phaethon could see his father from a distance each time he passed across the sky, Helios's home was far away and his daily task left no time for him to visit his child. If he had done so, the story of Phaethon might well have been a happier one, for as the boy grew up he was taunted by his companions. They did not believe him when he told them that the sun god was his father. They thought it was an idle boast, to cover up the fact that Phaethon's father had left home.

'You are no better than one of us,' they told him. 'We do not need to pretend that our fathers are gods to make us seem important. We are quite happy to be what we are and you should be too.'

'I will prove to you that you are wrong,' Phaethon said angrily, for he was proud of his father, and his mother had taught him always to stand up for himself in arguments. He thought for a while and decided that there was only one way in which he could show that he was telling the truth. He must visit Helios and ask of him a favour which, if granted, would leave no doubts in the minds of the other boys.

So he set off and after many days reached the place where his father's palace towered up beyond the eastern horizon.

'I am Phaethon, your son,' he said as soon as he came to his father. 'I have journeyed a long way, from the home of my mother Clyme in Egypt, to see the god who is my father, and to ask him a favour.'

Helios greeted his son warmly. 'You have only to ask,' he said at once. But when Phaethon told him what he wished to do, he frowned.

'What you ask is not possible,' he said. 'Ask anything of me but that. Skill and experience and great strength of arm are needed to do what you suggest. You are too young, still, to be entrusted with such a task.'

For Phaethon had asked his father if, for one day, he could take Helios's place and drive the sun chariot across the sky. His friends would see him and could not doubt that he had spoken the truth.

Phaethon pleaded and for a while Helios remained firm, but he had given his word and eventually he reluctantly granted the wish. 'Very well,' he said at last, 'but it must be for one day only. My horses are wild and untamed and, since time began, no one but myself has been entrusted to control them and hold them to their course. Go with great care; drive neither too high nor too low. Follow the broad path we have beaten over the centuries, and keep your hands always firmly on the reins. For if the horses are given their heads, disaster will surely follow.'

Dawn was approaching fast as Phaethon climbed into the sun god's chariot and took the reins in his hands. The horses seemed quiet and docile, and he felt confident as he cracked his whip and spurred them away into the clear night air. Up into the heavens they soared and as they went, their light first touched the tops of the hills in the east, spreading downwards to the valleys and to the villages crouching in the hollows below.

The horses tossed their heads and their golden manes streamed out behind them. A wild light came into their eyes as they felt once more the freedom of the skies, and sensed that the strong arm and iron will of Helios was not there to guide them. As they passed over Phaethon's homeland, he looked down and saw, far below, the tiny houses where he and his friends lived, the doors still firmly shut against the night.

'How will they know me?' asked Phaethon. 'I must take the horses down lower so that they will recognize me and see just what it means to have a god for a father.'

Cracking his whip over the horses' heads, he urged them downwards, away from the path beaten across the sky by a million journeys, down towards the earth. The horses plunged wildly, diving down closer than Phaethon had intended, so that the trees and rocks seemed to swoop up at him, then away, as the chariot veered suddenly sideways and up again. From the corner of his eye he saw a panic stricken group of his friends cowering beside his house, then they disappeared from view again as the fiery chariot dipped and rolled.

By now the horses knew that they were the masters. They skimmed low over the earth's surface, searing the trees and grasses, withering the corn, and setting cities ablaze with the terrible heat of the sun: the fertile land of Egypt became a red, barren desert, except for a thin thread of green where the Nile waters flowed. For a time even the great river itself shrank to nothing as the water boiled and steamed. The next minute, the horses were galloping high at the edge of the sky itself while the earth below grew cold and the seas froze into great blocks of ice.

Phaethon cried out to his father for help, but the sun god could do nothing. It seemed that the whole earth must perish. And so it might have done had not Zeus, watching always from Olympus, siezed one of his thunderbolts and hurled it with deadly aim at the boy.

Phaethon fell from the chariot with a great cry and plunged down to earth, falling to his death at a place called Eridanus. There, water nymphs wept with sorrow, cooling his burned body with their tears, trying in vain to revive him. It is said that Zeus took pity on the mourners and turned them into poplar trees, their tears into drops of amber. There they stand for ever, sighing in the wind, cooling the earth around them with their fluttering leaves.

Helios set out sadly to look for his runaway chariot. He found it high in the mountains of Ethiopia, parching the land for miles around as the four horses stamped and whinneyed in confusion. Helios threw his cloak over their wild eyes to calm them and led them quietly back to their stable in the west, flying slowly and carefully, high above the usual path. And for the rest of that day, darkness covered the land.

Athene, goddess of wisdom

It seems unlikely that Zeus was ever bored. Not only did he spend much of his time trying to keep order among the very temperamental gods, he was also usually busy pursuing some nymph or even a pretty mortal girl. Hera was, of course, his principal wife, but she was not the only one. Metis, one of the old Titan gods, was also once his bride.

Metis married Zeus only after a long, reluctant courtship. First she turned herself into a fish to escape from him, but he also became a fish and swam after her. She leaped from the water into the air and became an eagle, and Zeus became an eagle, too. There was no escape. Soon the resigned Metis told Zeus that she was to bear him a child. Anxious to know whether it would be a son or a daughter, Zeus consulted the oracle at Delphi.

'Oh mighty Zeus,' the oracle proclaimed. 'The first-born child of Metis will be a girl of many gifts, talented, wise and good. But beware: should Metis bear a second child, it will be a son who will overthrow you, just as you overthrew the once all-powerful Cronus.'

Zeus was very displeased to hear this. He decided that he would take no risks, even with the first child. One day, before the baby was born, Metis was strolling in the gardens near Lake Triton in Libya. Zeus beckoned her to him. She approached, smiling, expecting a caress, but without warning Zeus seized hold of her and swallowed her as a pike swallows a tiny minnow. No child by Metis would live to threaten his reign of power.

Metis was gone, but in her place came a raging headache. None of the usual remedies would cure it, so Zeus sent urgent word to Hephaestus, the smith god, to come to him.

'There is an evil spirit inside me which must be released,' he said. The smith god, taking a great hammer which he had brought with him, drove a wedge into Zeus's skull so that the spirit could escape through the hole which it made. But no evil spirit came forth. Instead, from the top of Zeus's head there sprang a handsome young girl, with fair hair and the bluest of eyes, dressed in armour and holding a spear in her hand. From her looks, Zeus knew that this was Metis's child. Despite his earlier fears Zeus could not reject his beautiful daughter. He called the girl Athene.

Athene grew to womanhood in the place where she had come so strangely into the world. As the oracle had foretold, she was indeed gifted and seemed to have been showered with all the most sought-after qualities. Much of her knowledge she passed on, and from her

man learned many arts. She was the first to spin wool and from it make woven cloth, and she showed man how to make the wheel, the axe, the flute and the trumpet, the plough, and sails for the swift Greek ships. If a difference of opinion or even a fierce argument arose among those about her, Athene would usually manage to settle it by reasoned debate. Many times she was asked to sit in judgement at the court of Areopagus, for it was known that her verdicts would be just and, if possible, merciful.

Though Athene had a peaceful disposition, her skill in the strategy of war was put to the test on a number of occasions. However, she would always try first for a settlement by other means, as she did when Poseidon tried to claim Athens from her. Only in one matter did Athene show any weakness. She, like almost all the gods, could be jealous of rivals who tried to match her in any field in which she thought she was supreme and on one occasion she let jealousy influence her strongly.

At that time there was a young girl called Arachne living in Lydia, a land famous for its weavers and for the purple dye they used for much of their cloth. Arachne, though she was no more than seventeen, was the most skilful of them all as she worked at her loom. Not only was she quick and neat, but she was far more imaginative in the creation of new designs than any of her fellow workers.

As her skill grew, Arachne became more ambitious. She conceived a plan for a huge tapestry which would be her masterpiece. Into it she wove scenes from the stories of the gods, of Poseidon riding the waves in his chariot, of Demeter weeping for Persephone, of Prometheus chained to his rock with the terrible eagle's wing casting a shadow over him, of the beautiful Aphrodite, and of Artemis with her silver bow. These and many more of the immortals seemed to move across the tapestry as if they had a life of their own.

At last her work was finished. People came from all over the village to stare in wonder at the tapestry and word of its beauty soon spread from village to village and from town to town across the land of Lydia and beyond its borders. Arachne, already confident of her skill, grew proud and vain with all this admiration. When people praised her work, telling her it was a gift from Athene herself, she tossed her head. 'Not even Athene can match my work. Oh yes, she

showed me the first simple stitches, but look what I have done with them: I have created a work of art that even the gods will envy.'

Before long, Athene, sitting working at her own loom, heard the news. She decided to see for herself what the Lydian girl had done, and she appeared at once in the market-place of the village where Arachne lived. There the tapestry was displayed on two long tables. Athene wore no disguise and Arachne knelt before her, flattered that the great goddess wished to see her work, yet half regretting her boastful words. 'Rise, child, and show me what you have done,' Athene told her.

Slowly the goddess, with Arachne a few steps behind, moved along the tables where the tapestry lay, examining every stitch closely, noticing the blending of the colours, and the grand sweep of the design. As she looked, Athene's blue eyes seemed to darken and a frown creased the pale amber skin of her forehead. She had come expecting to see the work of a girl who might, if worthy, have become her pupil, but found instead a tapestry far finer than any she could have made herself.

Athene struggled not to let her feelings show, but she was a true daughter of the tempestuous Zeus, and the passionate jealousy which he had passed on to all his children could not be held in check. Her face contorted with anger, Athene seized the tapestry and, with the strength of great rage, ripped the cloth again and again until it lay in pieces on the ground.

White-faced, Arachne watched and then turned away and wandered into the woods. She could not bear to live any longer and hanged herself with her girdle from a branch of one of the trees,

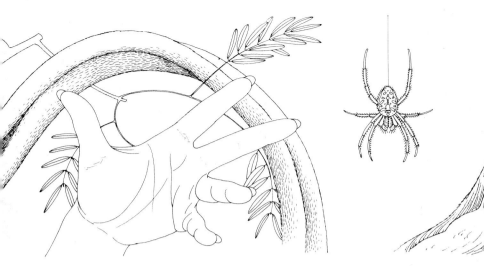

a sad, white-robed figure who had lost everything she valued. Athene followed. Half regretting her jealous rage she touched the dead girl.
'Weave on, little girl,' she said, 'but weave now for yourself alone. Your thread will now be a thousand times finer, your work a thousand times more delicate; but only a few people will stop to notice it, and no one, I think, will compare you with the immortals.'

As she spoke, Arachne's body dwindled and shrivelled, until the white dress hung like an empty shell from the tree branch. From its folds a tiny spider dropped soundlessly to the ground and immediately began unreeling its silken thread. From that day to this, Arachne the spider has woven her webs. Many lie dusty and forgotten in hidden corners, but in the early summer mornings you can see them sparkling and dancing in the sun, as fine as any garment of the gods.

Athene, like Artemis, did not marry; though many of the gods tried to gain her hand in marriage, none succeeded. However, Athene was more understanding than the cold goddess of the hunt. A man, Tiresias, once surprised her bathing, just as Actaeon had found Artemis. Artemis turned Actaeon into a wild beast to be hunted down. Athene punished her intruder with blindness, but gave him instead the gift of inward sight so that he became the greatest prophet of his time.

Athene is sometimes known as Pallas Athene, but there is some doubt as to how she came by this other name. There are several versions of the story and the first goes back to her very early youth in Libya. Even at that early age, she displayed many of the qualities which were to make her, as a woman, such a fine leader in war,

and many of the games which she played with her companions were mock battles. Unwisely, they were allowed small but realistic spears and swords to make their fights as real as possible. One day they became, tragically, too real.

Athene and her friend Pallas were down on the shore of lake Tritonis, dressed for their favourite pastime as warriors, with helmets, breastplates and shields. They would, they decided, be two of the Olympian gods, fighting for the hand of the fairest maiden the world had ever seen. They took their guard, sword in one hand, spear in the other, and then began to circle round, each one looking for an opening to attack. Athene saw her chance first and thrust with her spear. Pallas dodged, but at that moment Athene stumbled and Pallas was unable to move quickly enough out of the way. There was a cry and Pallas fell, pierced to the heart. From that day Athene put Pallas's name before her own, in memory of her friend.

In another version, the events took place when Athene was older, and had moved from Libya to Athenae on the Greek mainland. Again it is the tale of an accident, and again Athene and Pallas were sparring. But Pallas in this story has become Athene's foster-sister and the girls are being brought up by Pallas's father, the river god, Triton. Zeus, as ever, watched over the girl who had always been his favourite child, and when he saw that Pallas was about to make a winning thrust, distracted her attention. As she looked away, Athene's counter-thrust went home and Pallas was mortally wounded. It is the same story, really, and led to the same result – if Pallas ever existed. It could be that the name was simply given to Athene because it comes from the Greek word for girl.

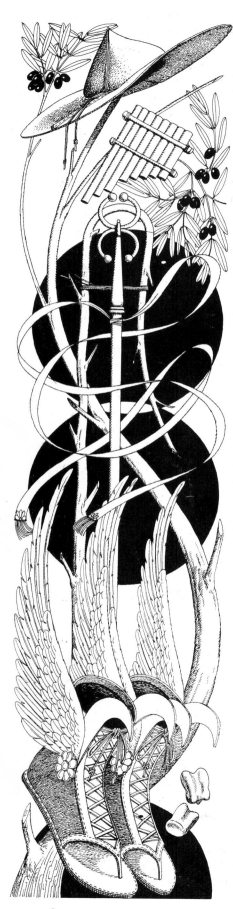

Hermes, the messenger of the gods

Many of the gods performed the most amazing feats when they were young but none of them could match the infant Hermes. He was born on Mount Cyllene, a son of Zeus and Maia, Atlas's daughter. It is said that he set out on his adventures when he was only a few weeks old – and for a god nothing is impossible. As he made his way down the mountainside, he saw below him a herd of white cows grazing in the valley, and his eyes lit with a mischievous gleam. Many who later crossed his path would come to know this expression well. He chuckled in his babyish way at the trick he planned to play on the owner of the cows.

Reaching the valley, Hermes cut a switch from an alder tree growing beside a stream, and used it to drive the cows into one corner of the meadow where they were grazing. As soon as they were penned there, he went back to the stream and cut long reeds from the waterside. He then carried these back to where the cattle stood, gathering bundles of grass as he went. With the reeds, he bound grass around the hooves of each cow and then drove them up a path into the mountains. Hermes knew that nobody would be able to tell which way they had gone, for the muffled hooves left no marks on the dusty, stony surface of the path.

They climbed upwards for some time, until Hermes saw below him a narrow ravine. Its sides were so steep that the bottom was in perpetual shadow, and, half hidden by a grove of olive trees, he spied a narrow path which led downwards into it. The descent looked perilous, but Hermes knew that in the ravine he had found a perfect hiding place for the cows. No one looking down from above would consider it a likely place for cattle to stray, and the gloomy shadows cast by the high walls would make it difficult to see them.

He led them in single file down the steep path. There was lush grass growing beside the small river that wandered across the floor of the ravine and, leaving the cows grazing contentedly, Hermes went on his way, delighted with the success of his plan. Whoever owned the cows would spend many a weary day searching them out.

What Hermes did not know was that the cows belonged to his half-brother Apollo. When Apollo found that they were gone from the valley, he naturally imagined that an ordinary cattle thief had been at work. He summoned a group of satyrs to help him, and together they scoured the mountainsides. Their search spread further and further until one day, passing through Arcadia, Apollo heard the sound of sweet music coming from the mouth of a cave. He decided to investigate, for he loved music of any kind, and the tune he heard was being played on an instrument strange to him. He noticed, too, that on the rough grass near to the cave, the hide of a white cow was stretched to dry in the sun.

Thrusting aside a bush of golden-flowered broom which partly hid the mouth of the cave, Apollo looked inside. In the half-light he saw the nymph Cyllene nursing a young child and, wondering, he realized that it was this child who was making the music. There was no sign of any thieves.

'Tell me, how is it that one so young can have such great accomplishments?' Apollo asked.

'I am as amazed as you,' she answered. 'All I can tell you is that he was born somewhere round here and found wandering alone. I am acting as mother to him till his true mother is found.'

Apollo bent close and examined the instrument which the young Hermes was playing. It was formed from the shell of a tortoise, with three strings stretched across the concave side. When they were plucked, the strings produced clear, resonant notes.

'Where did he get this?' Apollo asked. He had noticed that the strings were made from cow-gut, and his suspicions were once more aroused.

'It seems he made it himself. He calls it a lyre,' Cyllene told him.

Hermes had realized by now that Apollo must have seen the skin outside the cave, and he knew that the god's suspicions were quickly turning into certainties. So far he had not spoken, hoping that Apollo would not realize that he was anything different from what he seemed – a small, innocent child. But now he thought that the joke had gone far enough.

'You must forgive me,' he said. 'It was just a joke and I meant no harm. I will return your cows to you – all except one, that is. I had to kill one to make the strings for my lyre. In recompense, the instrument shall be yours and I will teach you how to play it.'

Apollo decided to make the best of what, to someone less fond of music, would not have been a very good bargain and Hermes led him to the secret ravine where the cows still grazed. The child was pleased to meet one of the gods and became talkative, telling Apollo about his short, but eventful life. Apollo quickly realized that the famous father Hermes kept mentioning was Zeus and he took Hermes back with him to Olympus.

Zeus was secretly much amused when he heard the story of how the baby Hermes had tricked his half-brother, but he tried to look reproving. 'Such conduct is not fitting in a god,' he said. 'The gods do not steal nor do they tell lies. But now you are here, what are we to do with you? You obviously have a clever way of talking and have already shown a taste for adventure and travel. Perhaps we can make something of that.'

He spent a few minutes in thought and then told Hermes that from that time on he would be the messenger of the gods and guardian of the rights of travellers. He gave him a herald's staff with white ribbons twined about it and a pair of golden, winged sandals which would carry him swiftly on his missions. Hades came to see the newest of the gods, and appointed Hermes to conduct the dying to his underworld kingdom.

Hermes's quick mind was never idle. He looked at the stars and wondered about them, and the science of astronomy was born. He studied letters and made the first alphabet; he formed the first musical scale, invented weights and measures for grain and liquids, and he learned from the wise ones how to foretell the future. The game of knucklebones was his idea, and so were card games, though the cards were different from those we know today. Among many other discoveries, he found out how to make fire by twirling a hard-wood stick in a hole in the side of a dry rotten tree stump, and he taught this skill to others.

He was considered to be the god of herds, and also of business – and thieves. In those days, when cattle were a very important measure of a man's wealth, herds and business went naturally together; his protection of thieves was in keeping with his own mischievous nature.

Many admired his gifts and some envied his accomplishments. They laughed at his witty remarks, but they always reserved their judgement on the amazing stories he told of his exploits until further proof of their truth should be forthcoming. Gay, a good companion and an amusing talker he might be, but one could not wholly rely on what he said. He was rather apt to deceive, not by outright lies, but by half-truths. It was difficult to tell at times whether he was serious or joking, and the more solemn of the gods found this difficult to understand. To them, the kind of practical jokes which Hermes loved to play would only have been funny if they themselves had thought of them. With Hermes, they were apt to be the victims.

Pan and Dionysus, the wild gods

Many different people have been called the father of Pan. It goes almost without saying that they include the lively Zeus, but for once nobody can say for certain that it was he. The truth might well be that Pan was disclaimed by his real father because he looked so hideous: gross and hairy, he had the horns, beard, tail and legs of a goat. The other gods despised him because of his physical appearance and did not really count him as one of themselves, though by birth he probably was a god and, according to some, a god older than even the ancient Titans.

Pan did not seem to mind very much, for he was quite a simple being and not ambitious. He did not aspire to the lofty heights of Olympus, but was content to live instead with the mortals in Arcadia in the centre of southern Greece. This was a land of open plains, interspersed with woods and forests. To the north there were tall mountains where Pan lived the life of a herdsman and shepherd, looking after his sheep and goats and tending his bees. At night, he joined enthusiastically in the revels of the nymphs of the woods and hills. At these times a certain wildness came over him. He loved nothing better than to hide away among the trees when a stranger was passing by and to terrify him with a sudden, unearthly cry.

Pan wooed many of the nymphs, among them Syrinx, who fled in horror to the banks of the river Ladon and turned into a reed to escape him. Unable to single her out among so many, Pan cut a number of the reeds and from these he made the pipes by which he is known to this day.

It was only when his great skill as a piper became known that the gods brought Pan to Olympus for a while to teach them his art. But he soon learned from their mocking looks that they did not want him for himself, and he returned once more to Arcadia and the life he knew.

The story of the god Dionysus contrasts starkly with that of the contented, unambitious Pan. It is a story of madness, plunder and pillage, of a god driven by forces he could not control.

Zeus was Dionysus's father and Semele, daughter of the king of Tyre, was his mother. Zeus's jealous wife, Hera, destroyed Semele with lightning, but the Titan goddess Rhea carried the new baby safely away into the care of King Athamas of Thebes and his wife Ino. For extra safety, Dionysus was disguised as a girl while he was with them. Despite this, Hera traced his whereabouts and brought madness on the royal couple so that they killed their own children in a frenzy.

For the moment, Dionysus himself was not harmed, but at Zeus's command, Hermes travelled swiftly to Thebes and turned the boy into a goat in order to hide him better. Then Hermes took Dionysus away secretly by night to Mount Nysa, where the nymphs could watch over him. With them, he regained his human form, save for two small horns, like those of a young kid, which remained with him for the rest of his life. It was while he lived on the mountainside that he cultivated the first vine and made a vineyard on the steep southern slopes. He was to plant vines wherever he went throughout his life, and would eventually be known as the god of wine.

For a while everything seemed to be going well, but Hera had not given up her search for the boy and at length she found him. Showing no mercy, she twisted his brain so that he became mad, just as she had done with Athamas and Ino.

Dionysus now rejected the gentle nymphs who had looked after him with such loving care. Instead, he chose as his companions the rough, unruly satyrs, led by Silenus, and the maenads. The maenads were wild, untamed women with wickedly gleaming eyes. Dressed in animal skins and armed with swords and serpents, they were terrible to look at, and destroyed anyone who came in their way.

With this strange band of followers, the young god roamed far overseas, fighting battles and slaying without pity everyone who crossed his path. First he visited Egypt, where the Amazons joined forces with him to restore King Ammon to his throne. Then came a long journey overland to India, where many bloody battles were fought until the whole land was subdued. In the east, Dionysus saw many sights, customs and creatures unknown at that time in the land of his birth, and he brought back with him to Europe the first elephants for western man to wonder at.

On Dionysus's return, Rhea defied Hera and drove the madness from him, but it seems that she was too late. Though somewhat changed, Dionysus would not give up his band of satyrs and maenads and the kind of life which they had lived together. He had grown too fond of their common bond – their love of revelry and wild living – and of the wine made from the grapes he planted and tended.

Dionysus and his strange army, though they lived for fighting, were not always victorious. Lycurgis, king of the Idonians, defeated them outright when they invaded Thrace, and though the watchful Rhea turned Lycurgis mad to save

Dionysus, he escaped death only by plunging into the sea. There the sea nymph Thetis hid him until danger was passed.

In a more peaceful mood, the wine god and his followers visited Thebes, the principal city of Boeotia, which lay some days journey north of Athens. The people there were quiet and reserved and, though they tried to be friendly, they were disgusted by the behaviour of the undisciplined, half-intoxicated satyrs and maenads. The local people viewed with disapproval the wild dancing that went on by night on the slopes of Mount Cithaeron above the town, and were kept awake at night by the sound of music from dusk to dawn.

The king of Thebes knew that some deference was due to a god, but his people had suffered too much; he ordered the arrest of Dionysus and his band of followers. Before it could be carried out, however, Dionysus sent him mad. The satyrs then escaped and went rampaging over the country, looting and killing.

Leaving Boeotia in turmoil, Dionysus set sail for the Aegean Islands. He boarded a ship bound for Naxos and was some days out when the rough-looking crew, unaware of his identity, seized him and bound him to the mast. Then they turned the ship eastwards towards the port of Priene in Asia Minor, where they planned to sell him as a slave.

They found very quickly that they had made a mistake, for Dionysus easily broke his bonds. For a moment he stood before them, his rather slight figure seeming to tower to twice its height. Suddenly, in his place was a snarling lion. A roaring, like that of a multitude of wild beasts, filled the air. Vines sprang from the deck and entwined the rigging, and the ship shuddered as if struck by a gigantic wave.

The sailors stood white-faced and petrified with fear. Then as one man they turned and fled, diving into the sea. There they became dolphins, leaping through the crests of the waves.

Turning the boat, Dionysus sailed once more for the island of Naxos. There he was to meet and marry a king's daughter and, perhaps because of her influence, his life ended more happily than it had begun. As time went on, he arranged the release of his long-dead mother from the Underworld, though he changed her name from Semele to Thyone so that Hera should not know what he had done. Such thought for others was new to Dionysus and showed that his evil days were behind him.

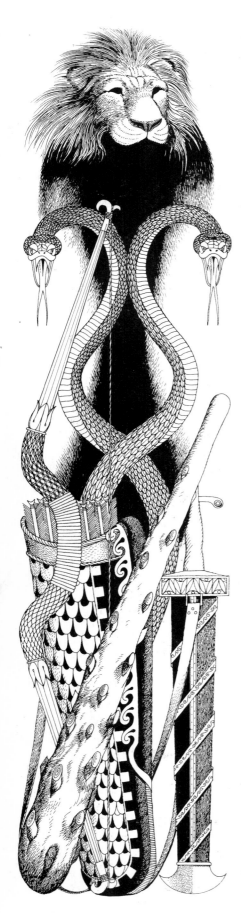

The labours of Hercules

Hercules is perhaps the best known of the Greek heroes and the stories about him and what he achieved are seemingly endless. In fact, there are so many that it is likely that the exploits of other, less popular men and gods were, in the course of time, attributed to him. If not, he was an amazing man indeed.

Zeus was Hercules's father, but his mother was Alcmene, a mortal woman. Hera resented the presence of yet another new baby about which she knew nothing and, full of vengeance, devised a plan to destroy the child. She decided to put two poisonous serpents in his cradle. However, though Hercules was only a few weeks old, he was already so strong that the serpents were no threat to him. He seized them in his fists, twisted them into a knot and so strangled them both.

Hera accepted defeat, for the time being, and Hercules grew into a youth of immense strength and physical courage. The celebrated athlete Polydeuces, whose story will be told later, trained him in the use of arms; from Autolycus, a son of Hermes, he learned to wrestle; and from Eurytus, grandson of Apollo, he learned to shoot with bow and arrows. He was instructed in the arts, too, and became a fine lute player.

Having mastered such a wide variety of accomplishments, the young man meditated for some while on how his life should be spent. One day, when he was walking on Mount Cithaeron, two women appeared before him. Their names were Pleasure and Virtue, and they offered him a choice. Pleasure offered a life of ease and plenty, Virtue a life of toil and struggle and some sorrow, but with the promise of glory at the end of it. Hercules chose Virtue, and immediately began looking for a worthy cause for which he could fight.

His first good deed was to relieve the city of Thebes of a heavy tribute it had been forced to pay to a neighbouring state. To show his gratitude Creon, the king of Thebes, gave Hercules his lovely daughter Megara. Hercules and Megara were happy together and soon had fine children. But the sorrow foretold by Virtue came all too soon. Hera saw her chance to strike once more and she drove Hercules mad, so that he imagined that Megara and his children were his enemies. In a terrible rage, he killed them all.

The madness passed and Hercules, grief-stricken, journeyed to Delphi to ask the oracle how he could atone for what he had done. 'Go forth to the city of Tiryns in Argolis, where Eurystheus is king,' said the oracle. 'There, for the span of twelve years, you must serve

Eurystheus. If you carry out faithfully all the tasks he gives you, forgiveness will come to you and your soul will be at peace.' So saying, the oracle fell silent and Hercules set out on his journey.

The first of the twelve tasks or labours which King Eurystheus set Hercules did not take him far from Tiryns. News had reached the palace that the countryside at Nemea, near Corinth, was being laid waste by a lion which came down from the hills each night, killing and maiming as it went. Both animals and men were its prey, and now the peasants of the area were too frightened to leave their homes, even when the sun was high.

'The lion must be killed,' Eurystheus told Hercules, 'and flayed, too. You must return with its skin as proof that it is really dead. But take the utmost care, for it is said that no weapon so far devised can penetrate its tawny hide.'

Hercules took his sword and spear and a stout club and, with a net of thick rope over his shoulder, he set off. Two days later, having learned from a terrified shepherd that the lion's lair was in a cave in the hillside not far distant, he made his way there. It was early morning, and Hercules crouched near some bushes by the cave's entrance to wait for the lion to return from its night's hunting. Presently it came over the brow of the hill, slinking from bush to bush, its great jaws dripping blood. Huge and powerful, the very appearance of the lion would have made most men turn and fly.

Undaunted, Hercules stepped out into its path, and as he raised his spear the lion paused. The spear whistled through the air, and the great beast sprang forward with a roar. But though Hercules's aim was true, the spear bounced harmlessly from the great beast's chest.

Dodging to one side, Hercules thrust his sword with all his strength at the lion's flank, but the sword had no more effect than it would have had on solid rock. Snarling with rage, the lion whirled and charged once more. Hercules rose to his full height and, throwing his useless sword to the ground, swung his club with all the strength he possessed so that it whistled through the air like a meteor descending. As the club struck, the gaping jaws of the lion snapped shut and it staggered under the blow. Dazed and for the moment afraid, the lion sped quickly into its cave before Hercules could take advantage of the damage he had done.

He had proof enough now that no ordinary weapon was any use against the lion: even his club could not subdue it. Hercules decided to try cunning. He fixed his net across the mouth of the cave and then crept inside through another opening in the rocks. Trapped in the narrow space, the lion roared defiance and backed into the net, for in the twisting passages of the cave it could not gather itself for a spring. Relentlessly, Hercules advanced and the earth trembled as the pair met; but the fight was brief. With a lightning thrust, Hercules's hands were on the lion's throat and after only a short, final struggle the lion lay lifeless before him.

He rested a while, wondering how he could flay the lion if no knife could pierce its skin. At last inspiration came. He severed one of the animal's own scythe-like, curved claws and used this to remove the skin. Then, wrapping it around him, he returned to Tiryns.

Lerna, not many miles from Argos, was a desolate place. A river ran through it and great swamps stretched out on either side. These swamps were the home of the Hydra, a monster with nine snake-like heads that preyed on any travellers who passed that way. Many warriors and hunters had tried to stalk and kill it, but without success. People said that when one head was cut off another at once grew in its place so that the monster was as strong as before. One head among the nine was immortal. It was against the Hydra that King Eurystheus next sent Hercules.

Dressed as he now always was in the skin of the Nemean lion, he set out in his chariot for the marshes, driven by a young woman called Iolaus. The wind whistled over the bleak landscape and the tall, plumed reeds bent before it. Sea-birds called in the distance.

The Hydra did not appear at once, but Iolaus pointed to a grove of plane trees on a neck of slightly higher land, where it was thought to have its home. Hercules fired burning arrows into the air, so that they fell among the trees and at once a great hissing sound drowned the cries of the gulls as the many-headed beast came writhing out from the trees, its forked tongues darting in and out and evil shining from every wicked eye.

Hercules advanced and struck at the Hydra with his sword. A head flew through the air, but instantly another began growing in its place. He struck again and yet again. Two more heads were gone, but two soon replaced them. In retaliation, the Hydra coiled itself about Hercules's legs to crush him. He fought fiercely on, but against such an enemy it was hard to see how he could win.

Alone by the chariot Iolaus watched – but there was another watcher, too: from far above, Hera looked down on the terrible struggle.
'I have waited long enough for a chance to avenge myself on Zeus,' she mused. 'His son shall now perish by my hand.' With these words she caused two giant crabs to crawl from the muddy waters of the marsh below, where the fight was taking place. Slowly they moved towards the fight and their armoured claws closed on Hercules's bare ankles. Their relentless grip would have crushed the bones of most men, but Hercules kicked the crabs away and brought his foot down on them with a hammer-blow that cracked their shells in two.

Now Hercules was tiring and he called Iolaus to his aid. She lit a torch of burning wood and, as Hercules severed one head after another with his sword, she seared the stumps which were left, so that new heads could not grow. Gradually the Hydra weakened, and with a last mighty sweep of his sword, Hercules cut off its one immortal head and stamped it into the soft earth until the fierce light of evil in its eyes shone no more. Being half a god himself, Hercules had the power to destroy an immortal. He dipped his arrows into the Hydra's venom to give them even greater deadliness against future enemies.

The third labour of Hercules was less demanding on his strength and courage, though it tested his patience and his skill as a hunter. It was to capture unharmed the hind of Ceryneia and to take it to Tiryns.

This hind was said to be one which had escaped when Artemis had sent out her hounds to find deer to draw her chariot. She had coveted it for its golden horns. After it had escaped, it went to live on the rocky lower slopes of the hills to the north of the province of Arcadia.

Day and night Hercules stalked the hind across the land, as spring turned to summer and autumn to winter. It seemed at first that its speed and cunning would keep it safe from Hercules as well as from Artemis. Then, as the spring flowers bloomed once more the hind grew weary. It had travelled many, many miles across plains and over mountains and still the relentless hunter pursued it. Exhausted, it lay down to sleep one night,

and was so tired that it did not wake at once when morning came. Hercules found it in a hollow in the hills and, creeping quietly to the spot where it lay, gently spread his hunting net over it. Thus he captured it unharmed and, as the king had asked, carried it home to Tiryns.
'You have done well,' said King Eurystheus, 'but I have a fourth task for you to perform when you have rested.'
'I need no rest,' Hercules told him. 'The pursuit of the hind was just gentle exercise and I am ready for what may come.'
'That is good,' said the king. 'For to capture the Erymanthian boar alive is something not to be undertaken lightly.'
'What is that?' Hercules asked, for he had been away so long, he had not heard of the latest troubles.
'News has come from a district far to the northeast, on the borders of Arcadia, where the river Erymanthus runs. A savage boar of enormous size has reduced the whole province to a state of terror. Its tusks are said to be the length of a man's arm, and it fears neither man nor beast. But it must, like the hind of Ceryneia, be taken alive.'

Next morning Hercules set out once more.

After five days he reached the river. There was no need to ask anyone where the wild boar might be, for there was snow on the ground and almost at once he was able to pick up its trail. The marks of its cloven hooves were so large that Hercules gripped his sword more tightly and looked warily about him as he followed the trail.

Soon he heard a restless movement and a loud snorting coming from beyond a thicket of leafless bushes. He stopped and stood silently looking about him. To the left of the thicket the snow lay deep, where it had drifted into a hollow. With great caution he crept to the right and, rounding the thicket, just had time to see that the boar was there before throwing back his head and letting out a nerve-shattering bellow. Not surprisingly, the boar, started into a panic, fled from him with a squeal of fear, heading directly away from him towards the hidden hollow. Next moment it was floundering helplessly in the deep snowdrift. It was the work of a minute for Hercules to cast his net over it and bind it fast with strong ropes. Taking its great weight on his broad shoulders, he carried it away.

King Eurystheus was not too pleased when he heard how easily Hercules had captured the boar. The tasks he set were intended to be almost impossible and the king thought hard before he decided what the next one should be. Finally he told Hercules that he must clean the stables of King Augeias in one day. On a visit to the king, Eurystheus had seen that many of the buildings were knee-deep in the droppings of cattle and horses, and great piles of dung filled the yards around them. Clearly, they had not been cleaned out for many years. Pestilence was spreading from the stables over the province of Elis, where Augeias ruled, but he was too lazy to do anything about it. He raised no objection when Hercules arrived and told him of Eurystheus's command, but he laughed when he heard that it was to be done in one day.

'One barrow-load alone will take an hour. A hundred – perhaps a thousand – barrows would be needed, and no day that I know of has a thousand hours in it,' he said.

Hercules smiled to himself. He had seen that the river Alpheus flowed near and already had a plan. He built a dam across the river, diverting its swiftly flowing waters so that they came rushing through the yards and stables, sweeping all the filth before them till not one scrap remained.

'Use your thousand barrows to carry the earth

from the dam, so that the river may resume its course,' Hercules told Augeias, with a twinkle in his grey eyes. Then he returned to Tiryns once again to find out what his sixth labour might be.

The king told him that many of the most skilled bowmen in Greece had recently returned from an unsuccessful raid on the haunts of the Stymphalian birds. These birds lived on the marshes that bordered Lake Stymphalus, in the shadow of Mount Cyllene, where Hermes was born. The birds, which were rather like storks, had claws and beaks of brass and could shed heavy, brass feathers from their wings at will. The falling feathers pierced the skulls of anyone they dropped on and the birds then swooped down to devour the body.

Because of the treacherous, boggy ground and the birds' wariness of strangers, it was almost impossible to come within arrow-shot of them. Moreover, they seemed to sense if a man were armed or not. If he was not, they would attack. If he was, they would keep away. Eurystheus told Hercules that the birds must somehow be driven from the land.

Armed with his bow and arrows, Hercules first tried stalking the birds in conventional fashion, inching his way through the thin reeds. However, under his weight the soft ground gave way to the oozing mud beneath it and he only just managed to scramble back in time to firmer ground. Away in the distance he could still see the birds moving on their stilt-like legs on the lake shore. They seemed not in the least worried by the presence of an intruder. Experience had told them that they were safe if they stayed where they were.

During the years of his labours, Hercules encountered the gods from time to time and sometimes they gave him help and advice. It happened that Athene was passing through Arcadia at this time and she reached Mount Cyllene while Hercules was there. He told her about his problem and she produced for him a huge brass rattle, which had been made for her by Hephaestus.
'It makes a noise like the crackling of a forest fire,' she told him.

Hercules was doubtful if this would have much effect on the birds, but as he could not think of anything else himself, he decided to try it. Taking the rattle, he climbed some way up the mountain until the whole lake lay spread out before him. He raised the rattle above his head and twirled it round and the birds immediately rose up from the further shore in a great cloud, startled by the strange noise. In panic they wheeled about, their harsh cries sounding their alarm, and then headed towards him. For a moment Hercules thought that they would attack him and he shot arrow after arrow into the air. A number of the birds fell, but the others passed high overhead and were soon lost to sight. By nightfall they had not returned. Hercules waited one day more to make sure that they did not come back, then went on his way to Tiryns.

Eurystheus's next order was that Hercules should capture an enormous, fire-breathing bull which was running free on the island of Crete, destroying crops and goring people who got in its way. It was said to have sired the monstrous Minotaur, half man, half bull, which was imprisoned on the same island. Hercules's task was to capture the bull and bring it to Tiryns.

So Hercules set out on a long sea crossing to the island of Crete, where he was welcomed by King Minos in his city of Knossos. Minos told him how the people of Crete could not venture from the city without risking their lives, and how grateful he would be if Hercules could capture the bull.
'If you are in need of help, you have only to ask. Anything you need shall be provided instantly,' King Minos told him.

Hercules knew that the bull, formidable though it might be, had no magical powers. He thought his own agility and strength should be more than a match for it, provided always that he could escape the searing blast of the fire which came from its nostrils. He found the bull easily, just outside the city walls, and leaped sideways as it charged. As it went past him he sprang on to its back, seizing its horns and wrestling it to the ground. Soon its legs were firmly bound and, flexing his shoulders, Hercules lifted it up bodily and carried it to where his ship was anchored in a harbour near the capital.

Minos gratefully wished him farewell and Hercules set sail for Nauplia, the nearest port to Tiryns on the mainland of Greece. Once back in the city, Hercules delivered the bull to King Eurystheus, who unwisely let it go free. In the course of time it wandered northwards, passing the great fortress of Mycenae and crossing the isthmus that joins the northern and southern parts of Greece at Corinth. Finally it settled on the plain of Marathon on the coast near Athens, where it began a new reign of terror which lasted

until another hero, Theseus, finally destroyed it.

By this time, however, Hercules had set out from Nauplia at the start of his eighth adventure. He travelled by ship far to the north, to Thrace, a land ruled by the fiery king Diomedes. The journey lasted many days, some of fair weather, some of wild storms. The ship sailed up through the Aegean Sea until it landed at the Thracian port of Abdera. From there, Hercules travelled overland to the capital, Tirida.

Diomedes was friendly, but Hercules was on his guard, for Eurystheus had warned him what to expect. The king of Thrace was a fine warrior, but wild and cruel in his ways: he fed the mares which he harnessed to his war chariot on the flesh of those he conquered in battle. When he was not fighting, the mares still had to be fed and the king's solution to the problem was to order his guards to cut the throats of the palace guests. Their bodies were then placed in the mangers of the royal stables where the mares tore them greedily limb from limb. Hercules was to tame the mares and take them back to Tiryns. First, however, he had to avoid the usual fate of Diomedes's guests.

He decided to lose no time but to act before Diomedes could suspect the purpose of his visit. He went to bed early on his first night, but lay with his sword by his side and did not sleep. The hours passed slowly, but no one came to molest him and just before dawn he rose and crept quietly from his room. He made his way down a long passage, to a side door which he knew was guarded by a single sentry.

The man was dozing at his post and Hercules overcame him quickly before he could cry out. Then he stole like a shadow to where the stables stood, a dark mass against a sky which was beginning to lighten with the approach of day. The grooms who tended the mares were, like the sentry, half asleep and Hercules overpowered them one by one until all lay senseless on the ground. So far things had gone well, but he knew that the hardest part of his task was yet to come.

The four mares were tethered in their stalls by iron chains and these would have to be broken before they could be set free. Hercules could hear the mares moving restlessly, for they scented the presence of a stranger and were growing alarmed.

Hercules knew that he could snap the restraining chains, using the strength of his arms alone, but to attempt this he would have to go close to the mares and risk being torn to pieces or kicked to death by them. He must find some way of keeping out of range of those death-dealing jaws and flying hooves. He looked about him and in the growing light spied a woodman's axe by the door. This was just what he wanted.

He fetched it and then stood near the end stall. He could see that the chains which held the mares were linked to iron staples driven into oak uprights, the tops of which vanished into the shadows under the roof. Hercules braced himself and raised the axe above his head.

As the axe fell, the first staple went flying, wrenched from the wood. The startled mares reared and plunged, but before they realized what was happening, the axe was swinging at the

second staple, and again, and yet a fourth time, before Hercules darted clear. The mares were free and, trailing their chains behind them, they milled about terrifyingly in the confined space. But it was only a moment before they made for the doorway with a clatter of hooves loud enough to wake the dead.

Certainly they woke Diomedes and his guards, who came running down to the stables as Hercules raced after the mares to drive them on to a piece of high ground. A long inlet from the distant sea curled round three sides of the hill, and Hercules quickly cut a channel so that water completely surrounded it and rushed in a flood over the strip of land the guards were crossing in pursuit. They turned to flee, but Hercules sprang over the flood and, outrunning them easily, felled them one by

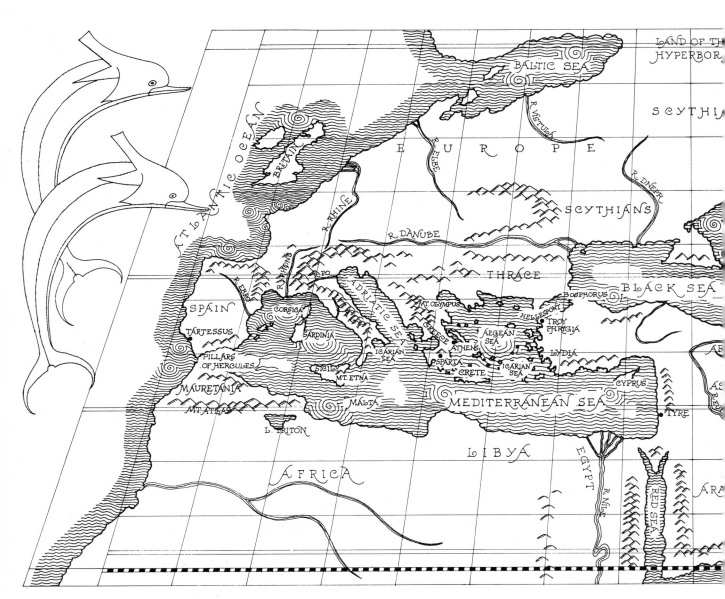

one with blows from his axe. Finally even Diomedes himself lay dead, and Hercules dragged his body to the hilltop, where his own mares devoured his body. Their hunger appeased, they became sufficiently docile for Hercules to bind their jaws with strong cord before driving them back to his ship for the journey home to Tiryns.

Hercules's ninth labour was to bring back to Eurystheus the golden girdle of Hippolyte, queen of a race of Amazons who lived on the shores of the Black Sea. Once more it was a long voyage, but eventually Hercules landed safely. At first Hippolyte offered him the girdle as a gift in token of her esteem and everything seemed to be going well. However, at this point Hera decided to interfere once more. She spread a rumour that Hercules's true purpose was to seize Hippolyte herself and carry her off. Angry at this supposed deception, the Amazons took up arms. Hercules soon put them to flight, but during the fighting he killed Hippolyte with his sword. Sorrowful that he had been misjudged and at the unexpected outcome of his visit, Hercules took the girdle and set sail once more for Nauplia.

For his next task, Hercules had to steal a herd of oxen from Geryon, the king of Tartessus on the Spanish peninsular. Geryon was a frightening figure: above his thick waist he had three bodies, each with its own arms and head. To get to Spain, Hercules borrowed the golden bowl which Helios the sun god used to return to his palace in the east after his daily journey across the sky. As he passed through the narrow straits which

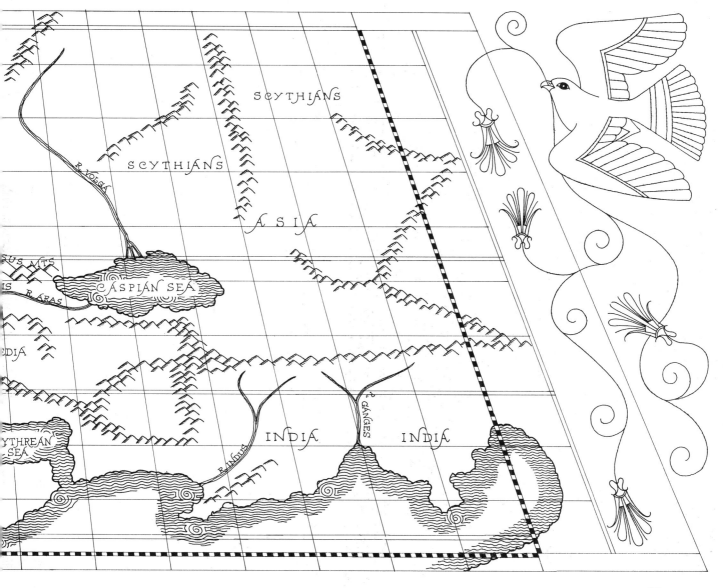

separate Spain from Africa, Hercules set up two great pillars of rock, one on either continent, to show he had passed that way. To this day they are known as the Pillars of Hercules. Then he set off overland to Tartessus, where Geryon kept his oxen pastured on a hillside under the care of a herdsman, Eurytion, and a fierce, two-headed dog called Orthrus.

Hercules killed the dog, Orthrus, with one arrow, and Eurytion with another. He was driving off the oxen when Geryon himself appeared and started to pursue him. However, Hercules hid behind a rock and, as the king drew level with him, fired at him from the side so that a single arrow pierced all three bodies and Geryon fell dead.

With the oxen beside him in the golden bowl, Hercules sailed once more for Greece, his tenth labour completed.

'Next, you must bring back to me apples from the tree of Hesperides,' Eurystheus told him. 'The tree stands in a garden on the slopes of Mount Atlas in the province of Mauretania, beyond the Libyan Sea.'

Hercules knew that this apple tree had been a wedding gift to Hera and that it was guarded by a fierce dragon. To defy Hera by taking her gift was a great risk, but Hercules thought that if necessary he could call on Atlas for aid. The Titan god crouched on the mountain-top above the orchard, eternally bearing the weight of the heavens on his massive shoulders. His daughters tended the garden where the apples of Hesperides grew and Hercules had been advised that the girls should gather the apples for him, but that he should not attempt to do so himself.

He arrived in Mauretania and killed the dragon. Then he climbed the mountainside near the garden. Above him towered Atlas and Hercules explained why he had come.

'My daughters will gladly fetch you some apples,' Atlas said, 'but I must find them first to tell them.'

'Can I not search them out?' Hercules asked. The Titan shook his head.

'It might take you many days,' he said. 'I know the most likely places to find them and if you will take my heavy load for just a short while I will fetch them to you with the least possible delay.'

So Hercules took the burden of the heavens on his own back and Atlas set off down the mountain. The daughters must, after all, have been close by, for Atlas soon returned with the two girls,

who carried with them a basket of the precious apples. Hercules was impatient to be on his way but Atlas, enjoying the first freedom he had had for many, many years, was not anxious to change places with him once again. Hercules began to suspect that the god had had other reasons for offering to fetch the girls himself. The longer Hercules shouldered the Titan's load, the less keen Atlas would be to take it back.

'When I have rested a while, you can go,' Atlas said, but he did not sound as if he really meant it. His voice was hesitant, like that of a person who was not used to deception. Hercules decided that it would be best to appear to agree. He told Atlas that in its present position the load was badly balanced and uncomfortable, and if Atlas would take the heavens once more for a brief moment, he would prepare himself to take the weight better. So Atlas bent his shoulders and Hercules transferred the heavens to him again. It was only when Hercules set off with the apples down the mountainside that Atlas realized he had been tricked, and that his brief rest was ended.

Strangely, Hera did not interfere with Hercules this time, and he returned safely to Tiryns.

For his twelfth and last labour, Hercules had to visit the Underworld, and bring back Cerberus, the fierce hound which stood guardian there. Descending into a deep cavern near Sparta, Hercules, with Hermes as his guide, soon came to the dark, swirling waters of the River Styx. Charon the boatman was reluctant to ferry Hercules across, for only the souls of the dead were allowed to pass that way. Luckily, Hermes so confused Charon with persuasive arguments that at last he consented to ferry Hercules across. And so, seeing many terrible sights as he went, Hercules entered the Underworld, where Hades and Persephone sat upon their thrones.

'You may take Cerberus back with you to Tiryns for a short time if you can overcome him without the use of sword, spear or arrows,' they told Hercules, smiling at each other, for they did not think that he could succeed. However, when Hercules approached Cerberus, he simply took the skin of the Nemean lion from his shoulders and threw it at the three snarling heads, entangling them in its folds so that they were helpless. Gathering the dog in his arms, Hercules set off for the world above with a light heart: his twelve labours were completed, and the guilt from the death of his family was erased at last.

The adventures of Perseus

King Acrisius ruled over the land of Argolis, a kingdom situated on the coast of Greece to the west of Arcadia. The Saronic Sea washed its rocky north-eastern shores, and both Tiryns and Mycenae lay within its boundaries.

King Acrisius was overjoyed when his wife bore him a beautiful baby girl. They called her Danae and the king took counsel from an oracle to see what the future might hold for her. Acrisius was far from pleased by what he heard from the oracle, for it predicted that one day, many years hence, he would be killed by his daughter's son.

To try to prevent the oracle's words coming true, he resolved that Danae should never be allowed to marry. However, she was so beautiful to look at that the king knew that many men would come seeking her hand. When she grew up he had her confined in a tall tower of brass, with a ring of guards around it. No man, not even the guards, was allowed to look at her lovely face. Acrisius's precautions were very effective; no man did come near her, though many people were curious and rumours spread somehow about her beauty. The tall, windowless tower was no obstacle to the gods, however, and one night Zeus disguised himself as a shower of gold and came secretly to visit her. The guards, of course, knew nothing. All they saw was an unusually strong beam of moonlight shining on the tower walls as Zeus left, and perhaps the wind in the trees was louder than usual.

Presently, Danae bore Zeus a son, whom she named Perseus. Acrisius was furious, and also afraid, for he saw before him the baby about which the oracle had made such a terrible prophecy. As he could not bring himself to kill the child in cold blood, he thought of a plan which would end its life without the direct responsibility resting for ever on his shoulders. Danae, with Perseus in her arms, was brought before him.

'A daughter who has deliberately deceived me is no longer welcome in my house,' he told her.

Weeping, Danae pleaded. 'The baby is so little,' she said, 'and it is no fault of his that he was born. Cast me out if you must, but let me leave Perseus where he can be properly cared for.'

Acrisius did not speak. He turned away from her. Her words had moved him, but he knew that he must be firm if his own life was to be saved. He left the room and did not appear again as his servants carried out his orders. Danae and the baby were taken to the coast and there set adrift in a huge wooden chest. With neither food nor

water they had no hope of surviving long, even if the chest stayed afloat.

But once again Acrisius's plan did not work out as he had intended. The chest bore the two fugitives across the waves to the island of Seriphos. There Dictys, brother of the island's king, gave them shelter and looked after them.

Perseus grew to manhood at the court. Only one thing made him unhappy. The king, Polydectes, wanted to marry Danae. She did not like him and as Perseus sided with her against the king, Polydectes decided that he must be removed. Without the support of her son, Danae might in time be brought to submit to his wishes. He sent for Perseus and smiled at him in the friendliest fashion.

'I have something to ask of you,' he said. 'All young men welcome a challenge which will prove their manhood.' Perseus waited, and Polydectes went on: 'People say that you are too much in the company of your mother and the other women – that you are not manly as most men are. I know this is not so, but I want to give you a chance to prove it to others.'

None of this was true, but Perseus believed what the king told him.

'If this is indeed what they say,' he said, 'tell me what I must do.'

'If you were to slay the Medusa and bring back its head, it would prove beyond doubt that you are afraid of nothing.'

Perseus did not feel at all brave when he heard this, though he tried not to show his feelings. The Medusa was the most terrible of all the gorgons, monsters that dwelt in the land of the Hyperboreans. Armed with long, curved talons and fangs more deadly than those of the fiercest wolf, it had a mane of venomous serpents. Anyone who looked at its hideous face was turned instantly to stone. Perseus could not refuse the challenge, for his whole reputation seemed at stake.

'I will go,' he said, 'and I will bring you back the the monster's head.'

From above Zeus was watching. He was proud of his son and called on the other gods to give the young man what aid they could. From Hades he received a helmet, and from Hermes wings for his feet so that he could travel quickly; but Athene's gift was the best of all, though it was not immediately clear what it was for: she gave him a large shield, so smooth and fine that its mirror-like surface reflected everything before it.

'When you reach the place where the Medusa lurks, look at it only in this shield,' she explained to him. 'For if you gaze on the monster directly you will be turned to stone.'

The land of the Hyperboreans was far to the north, where the sun rose and set only once a year. Perseus flew there on the wings of Hermes, covering miles of sea with the speed of a swallow. It was a gloomy place with scattered rocks and stunted trees. As he walked the last lap of his journey, he saw beside the path, more and more frequently, the shapes of men turned to stone.

At a village he learned that the Medusa could be found nearby. It lived in a small hollow in a bleak stretch of landscape, surrounded by yet more petrified figures. No one went that way now, he was told; even animals and birds shunned the place.

The villagers looked at him with awe as he unsheathed the sickle with which he had armed himself and set off. Presently he could see ahead of him over open ground a ring of about twenty sad stone figures, and he guessed that it must be among these that the Medusa lay in wait.

Taking Athene's mirror-shield from his shoulder, he turned his back on the stone circle. Staring into the shield, he moved slowly backwards, step by step, over tussocks of rough grass.

Presently he could see something moving, low down among the stones. At first he could not tell what it was, but then he realized that the hollow where the Medusa lived was coming into view. What he could see were the snake heads of its mane, though the beast below them in the centre of the hollow was still invisible. No sound was to be heard.

Perseus crept closer still to the hollow, but then his toe accidentally kicked against a stone. It went rattling away from him down a small, rocky slope. At once the air was filled with a mighty roaring sound, and in the mirror Perseus saw the monster rise into view, its jaws agape and its evil eyes flashing.

He stood his ground and it seemed that the Medusa itself paused for a moment, perhaps baffled because the man in front of it had not been instantly turned to a pillar of stone. Then it advanced, crawling like some infernal octopus across the ground, its snake heads hissing hatred.

With his heart beating loudly, Perseus waited, crouched slightly forward, his legs braced apart, holding the sickle across his body at the ready.

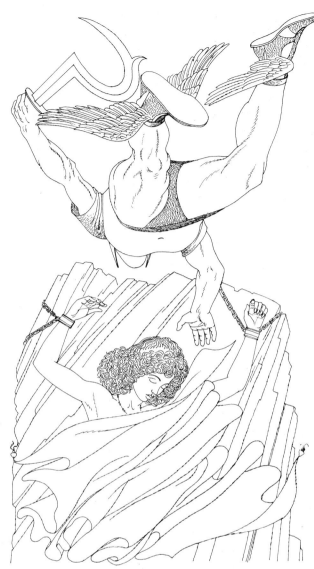

Even now he could feel the heat of the Medusa's fiery breath on his back. The shield reflected only its gaping mouth and gnashing teeth. Then, as if releasing a steel spring, he whirled his arm round and back. He felt the sharp edge of the sickle bite behind him and there came a terrible cry that seemed to shake the very rocks of the earth. Then all was still.

For a long moment Perseus stood without moving. Then he looked once more in the shield, for even in death the Medusa retained its power to petrify. The monster lay there on the ground, its loathsome head severed from its body.

Perseus had with him a sack of stout cloth and, reaching behind him, he lifted the head into it. Once it was in the sack, he tied the opening securely with cord, slung it over his shoulder and set out on his homeward journey. He walked at first so that he could spread the good news to the villages he had passed through. The people danced in the streets as he went. On reaching the coast, he used Hermes's winged sandals to fly out over the waves, keeping close to the rocky shoreline so that he would not lose his way.

He had covered many miles when, looking down, he saw far below him a tiny figure standing alone on a rocky outcrop which rose up from the sea. Thinking it must be a stranded sailor whom he could help to the shore, he swooped down and circled the rock, like one of the gulls which wheeled about it. But it was no sailor on the rock.

The figure he had seen, unclothed save for a necklet of fine jewels, was that of a beautiful, dark-haired girl, held fast to the rock by chains around her wrists and ankles. Landing lightly on a ledge beside her. Perseus covered her with his cloak and set about the task of breaking her fetters. Meanwhile, she told him her story.

The girl was Andromeda, daughter of Cepheus, a king of Ethiopia. Her mother had said often that both she and her daughters were fairer than any of the nereids, who lived beneath the sea and were renowned as the most beautiful of all creatures. Perseus nodded, for he could see that this might well be true of Andromeda. The mother had not been content to voice her opinion in the privacy of their home. She had told many others what she thought and how she despised the nereids. In time, word of what she was saying had reached the sea nymphs.

Jealous of their reputations, they had complained to their protector, Poseidon. He caused great waves to lash the shores of Cepheus's kingdom, so that they flooded the land. It was impossible for the people to escape, for the country was ringed by high mountains on the landward side and Poseidon had sent a scaly sea monster to patrol the coastal waters and prevent flight by sea.

Desperate, Cepheus consulted an oracle to find out how his land might be saved. 'Your daughter Andromeda must be sacrificed to the monster,' the oracle told him. 'Only in this way may Poseidon's wrath be appeased.'

Cepheus paled. 'Never! I will never allow that to happen,' he exclaimed in horror. 'I would rather lose my kingdom than my daughter!'

But he was not alone when the oracle spoke. Though they knew of Cepheus's great love for his daughter, his courtiers could not agree that she was more important than the rest of his subjects.

'So many should not be sacrificed for the sake of one,' they told him. 'We will sorrow with you if Andromeda should perish, for she is good and kind. But she must die if our land and our people are to be saved.'

His heart breaking, the king was forced to agree, and so Andromeda had been chained naked to the rock as Poseidon had demanded, waiting fearfully for the sea monster to come.

As she finished speaking she began to weep, but Perseus had no time to comfort her. Even now the monster might be on its way. He turned on the ledge and looked out over the white crests of the waves. It was fortunate that he did so, for even as he looked a horned head with staring eyes rose from the water and a long, serpent-like body, thick as the trunk of a tree, lashed the waves behind it.

Perseus leaped from the ledge high into the air and, expecting a direct attack, the monster turned towards him. It watched warily as Perseus circled, deciding what he should do. Suddenly the clouds above them parted, letting the sunlight stream through. This gave Perseus an idea. He would dive on the monster from out of the eye of the sun. Looking into its blinding light, the monster would not be able to see him until he had struck. He manoeuvred into position, and was about to dive when something happened which made him quickly change his plan.

The sun cast Perseus's shadow onto a wave beside the monster and its movement caught the beast's eye, deceiving it into thinking that a new enemy threatened it from the side. It half turned, and instantly Perseus dropped on it like a diving sea-bird. His sickle sliced through the air. The monster sensed the danger too late; its head flew from its body before it could turn to meet its assailant. Then the waves closed over it and it sank from sight.

As he flew back to the rock, Perseus could see that a ship was setting out from a small harbour a little way down the coast. Its red sails, billowing in the wind, caught the sunlight like a ruby and the seas frothed white about its bows. King Cepheus was already on his way to claim his daughter.

By now Perseus had fallen under her spell and knew that, whatever happened he must marry her. Andromeda seemed to feel the same and the king, in his gratitude to her deliverer, gladly gave his consent. The whole country rejoiced that everything had turned out so well and that their beautiful princess was once more among them. And so Perseus and Andromeda were married. But at the wedding feast which followed the ceremony the doors of the banqueting-hall burst violently open. A tall stranger stood silhouetted against the light, armed soldiers grouped around him.

'Stay!' he thundered. 'I claim Andromeda as *my* bride! Was she not promised to me? Speak, Cepheus! Is this not true?'

White-faced and speechless, the king could only nod in agreement, for what the stranger had said was indeed true. Perseus looked at Cepheus and saw that the king was in a predicament. He had let his joy at the return of his daughter sway his judgement and had overlooked the promise made earlier to the stranger, whose name was Agenor.

Perseus waited no longer. Vaulting the table, he attacked Agenor with his sickle. Agenor fell at the first stroke and his soldiers retreated under the fierce onslaught. The wedding guests scattered in panic and Perseus, seizing the frightened Andromeda by one hand and the sack with the Medusa's head in the other, ran down the stairs. No one dared to stop them, and very soon the palace was far away. On they sped till they reached some higher ground and Perseus, holding his wife in his arms, took to the air and headed out over the sea towards his home.

On the way, the pair rested a while in Mauretania, expecting a welcome from the god Atlas on his mountain-top, and from his two daughters. But their arrival was not well timed. For many months Atlas was able to resign himself to his task of supporting the heavens, with seemingly endless patience. But from time to time his bones would ache unbearably and he would think longingly of the brief spell when Hercules had taken his turn with the weight of the sky. Then he would be ill-tempered and moody. It was at such a time that Perseus and Andromeda arrived. Atlas would scarcely speak to them. He even ordered his daughters not to give them shelter.

Some say that it was pity that moved Perseus and some that he was angered at Atlas's unfriendliness to his new bride, but whatever the reason, he did a terrible thing. He took the Medusa's head from its sack and, keeping his own face averted, held it up for the mighty Titan to see. At once, Atlas was turned to stone.

Perseus and Andromeda continued their journey. Even when they eventually reached

Perseus's home, their troubles were not over. While Perseus had been away, King Polydectes had continued to pester Danae, thinking it certain that her son would never return. Danae had resisted, but she was almost alone in her struggle. The king's brother, Dictys, gave her what help he dared, but he could not defy the king directly. Eventually, wearied by Polydectes's persistance and seeing no other solution, Danae had reluctantly given way and consented to become his wife. The time of the wedding was fixed, and it was early in the morning of that very day that Perseus and Andromeda came winging from the skies. At her home, Danae was being robed by her attendants for the ceremony. Perseus found her weeping and she threw her arms about him.

'At last! At last my prayers are answered,' she cried. 'I could not believe that they would be in vain.'

She told him of Polydectes's demands and of the wedding which she had failed to prevent.

Full of rage, Perseus took the sack with the Medusa's head and strode through the streets to the royal palace. Polydectes too, was putting on his finery. He shrank back in fear when the young man burst through the doors of his robing room and confronted him. Slowly Perseus loosened the cords from the mouth of the sack while the king watched him, uncertain what to do.

He thought he saw his chance to attack when Perseus turned his head away, but Perseus was only making sure he did not see the terrible head he lifted from the sack. The Medusa's lifeless eyes gazed at Polydectes and, sword in hand, he was instantly as still as one of the stone statues which lined the halls of his royal home.

With the king dead, Perseus gave Dictys the throne and the island became a happier and more peaceful place. However, the prophecy that had been made by the oracle before Perseus was born had not yet been fulfilled and, indeed, had been almost forgotten. The time had come for the oracle's words to come true.

Although Perseus now lived quietly with his wife, he was still a young man and he liked to try his skill against other athletes. He was good at many sports, but best of all at throwing the discus, and was the acknowledged champion of the country.

Athletics played an important part in Greek life and, whenever games were held, teams would travel great distances to take part. Although they were called games, the gatherings were really for athletes, who competed against each other in running, wrestling, and with the javelin and discus. Such a contest was held one year in Argos, and Perseus went as one of his country's team.

The day came and the stadium was thronged with spectators. Banners flew from poles above the stands and as horns sounded a fanfare, the athletes from all the cities of Greece marched into the ring and formed in line to salute the elders. The chief of these was Acrisius, who, as king of that part of the country, had the place of honour. He had no idea that his grandson Perseus was among the athletes – indeed, he imagined that his daughter and her baby son had died long ago in the sea.

First one team then another competed in the different sports. Finally, it was time for the discus throwers to come on, and the crowds hummed with excitement as they took their stand at one end of the stadium. Perseus was the first to throw. As he swung round, his foot slipped on the grass, and the silver disc flew sideways from his grasp, skimming through the air towards the spectators. The heavy disc struck Acrisius on the head, killing him instantly. The oracle's prophecy was fulfilled: Acrisius had been killed by his own daughter's son.

The rival twins

Castor and Polydeuces and their cousins Idas and Lynceus, were two sets of twins. In fact, neither pair were true twins. Though Castor and Polydeuces had been born at the same time to the same mother, they had different fathers: Polydeuces was the son of Zeus, Castor the son of a Spartan king. In the same way, Idas was the son of Poseidon while Lynceus had a mortal father.

Castor and Polydeuces grew to be fine fighting men and great athletes, Castor as a charioteer and Polydeuces as a boxer. Together, they were known as the Dioscuri, and they won triumph after triumph for Sparta in the Olympic games. Idas and Lynceus also became good fighters and the four cousins were for a long time close friends. Their first quarrel was over women.

Idas and Lynceus were to marry two sisters. The very night before the wedding Castor and Polydeuces, who had naturally been invited, were out riding with the girls while their cousins made the final arrangements for the marriage ceremonies. Suddenly, they seized the reins of the girls' horses and galloped off with them over the hills to Sparta. Idas and Lynceus were outraged and for a long time the two sets of twins became bitter enemies.

After a time, Idas, at least, fell in love again, this time with a princess called Marpessa. Marpessa's father was a son of Ares, and he was very particular about her suitors. He devised a strange test to prove their courage. Each young man had to take part in a chariot race with him; the winner would take Marpessa, and the loser would die. As he was a champion charioteer himself, he felt confident that he could outdrive any of the young men who asked for her hand. Several took up the challenge and each time they were defeated easily. Marpessa began to think that she would never be married.

Then one day, a new challenger appeared, the god Apollo. Both Idas and Marpessa's father were afraid, though for different reasons. The father knew he could not win against a god, and Idas knew that he would lose his bride. Before the race could take place, Idas therefore stole Marpessa away in the middle of the night and carried her off to his home in Messene.

Apollo followed, and a fierce duel took place. Idas, though a son of Poseidon, was no match for Apollo, and it was only when Marpessa appealed to Zeus to intervene that he was saved. Zeus decreed that Marpessa should at last be allowed to choose her own husband, and, greatly daring, she defied Apollo and married Idas.

By the time all this had happened, Idas and Lynceus had almost forgotten their quarrel with the other pair of twins and on their next visit to Sparta, the four men finally made peace with one another.

'Why should two women come between us, when we are in other ways so close?' Idas asked. 'Perhaps so that they can snatch our purses to buy fine clothes for themselves,' said Castor, laughing.

'Or because we would not step out of their way when they wanted to pass,' added Polydeuces. 'At any rate, let us be friends,' said Lynceus.

Then the four cousins settled down to serious discussion, for Castor had a daring plan by which all four could greatly increase their stock of cattle. The plan was to raid the herds that grazed to the north of Sparta, on the plains of Arcadia. Having reached agreement, the four set off in two boats up the river Eurotas, taking their horses with them. In this way they completed a large part of their journey and arrived in Arcadia with their mounts fresh and ready for action.

The raid itself proved easier than they had expected. Almost at once they saw a herd of cows some two hundred strong, tended by only a few herdsmen. The herdsmen fled in terror as the four armed strangers rode towards them. The twins easily rounded up the cattle and drove them to a hidden valley in the hills some miles away. There they planned to keep the cattle concealed until all signs of pursuit had ceased, for they knew that although the herdsmen had run off, they would report the raid and there would be an armed search party.

'One thing we have not decided,' Idas said as the four men sat by their tent a few nights later, 'and that is how we should divide the cattle amongst us.'

'I presume that as we have shared the danger equally, we will divide the cattle in the same way. In other words, Idas and I will take half the herd.'

'But the original idea was mine,' pointed out Castor. 'Polydeuces and I should have the larger share.'

Idas and Lynceus would not, of course, accept this. The four argued for a while but could not agree. At length Idas suggested a plan to settle the matter in a way which would be fair to everyone. He killed one of the cows and divided it into four equal portions with his hunting knife. 'Each one of us will eat his own portion of meat,' he explained. 'The person who finishes his portion first wins half the cattle, and the one who comes second takes the rest.'

He had scarcely finished speaking when he began to gulp down his share and in an incredibly short time it was all finished. His twin Lynceus was hardly slower, and the Dioscuri were left hopelessly behind. There could be no doubt about who had won the cattle. Trying hard to hide their anger, Castor and Polydeuces watched their cousins drive the herd out of the valley and head south-east for Messene.

Castor and Polydeuces made their way back to the boats, their resentment growing stronger with every step. Before they reached the river, their minds were made up. They had shown friendliness, but it had been spurned. Once more the feud was on, and this time it would be a very bitter one indeed. Castor and Polydeuces vowed to retrieve all the cattle, not only those which were rightfully theirs. Even if it meant a fight to the death with the other twins, it would be worth it to claim revenge.

They turned their horses away from the river and headed in the direction their rival twins had taken. They arrived in Messene by night when Idas and Lynceus were already asleep, resting after their dusty journey with the cattle. Castor and Polydeuces drove off the herd and hid it once more. They knew that this time a more thorough search would be made, a search that would continue until the missing cattle were found. Idas and Lynceus would have no doubts about who was responsible and all the old hatred would be revived. The only thing was to strike by surprise, and the Dioscuri decided that when Idas and Lynceus came looking for them, they would be lying in wait for them.

The sun was just rising when they left the cattle and started back along the road to Messene, looking around them all the time for a likely place to hide. A little over a mile from the town they saw a graveyard beside the road. Tombstones rose up from the rank grass and there was an ancient oak tree not far from the path. Its trunk was broad enough to serve as a hiding place for one of them. Castor moved quickly in behind the tree while Polydeuces crouched nearby, close to the ground, in the shadow of one of the tall headstones. Everything seemed ready for a surprise attack.

However, unknown to Castor and Polydeuces, the theft of the cattle had been discovered during the night and Idas and Lynceus had already been

out searching for some hours, moving round the outskirts of the city, trying to pick up the trail. When daylight came, they soon found the hoof-marks on the Sparta road. They moved cautiously from cover to cover, expecting enemies in every bush. When Castor and Polydeuces appeared in the distance, they had just reached the graveyard themselves. They, too, decided that it would give ideal concealment and, bending low, they made a dash for the long grass and dropped down behind two of the headstones which were furthest from the road.

They could hardly believe their good luck as they watched the other twins, completely unaware of their presence, choose the same hiding-place, not ten paces in front of them and crouch down facing the path along which they expected the search party to come.

As soon as Castor and Polydeuces had settled down to wait, with their weapons beside them on the ground, Idas rose to his full height. Castor sensed the movement behind him and whirled round, but Idas's spear was already cutting through the air with its message of death. Before Castor knew it, it struck, piercing him to the heart and pinning him to the oak tree which he had thought would give him shelter.

Only seconds behind his brother, Lynceus launched his own spear at Polydeuces. His aim was not so true, and the spear glanced harmlessly off the gravestone behind which Polydeuces was crouching. Before Polydeuces could make a move, however, Lynceus seized one of the great stones and wrenched it from the ground, to send it hurtling through the air after the spear.

Polydeuces tried desperately to ward off the stone with his shield, but it came crashing through his guard and struck him on his left arm, splintering the bone. Wild with pain, and furious at the murder of his brother, Polydeuces rushed on Lynceus like a madman. Few could have withstood such an onslaught and after two lightning thrusts of Polydeuces's sword, Lynceus, too, lay dying.

Idas, seeing that Polydeuces's strength was ebbing as the blood flowed from his wounded arm, now rushed to the attack, expecting an easy victory. As it happened, things turned out very differently. As he moved forward, the whole graveyard was lit by a blinding flash of light and when Polydeuces uncovered his face, it was to see Idas lying sprawled on the ground. His sightless eyes stared towards the sky as smoke drifted over him and billowed away among the gravestones. Zeus, watching the combat from above, had saved his son with a thunderbolt.

Of the two pairs of ill-fated twins, Polydeuces was the only one now left alive. He managed to carry Castor's body to the place where he had hidden the horses and to lay it over his saddle. Then, slowly the sad journey back to Sparta began. The herd of cattle grazed forgotten by the roadside.

Polydeuces buried Castor with all the honour due to a king's son, and a fine monument was set up in his memory; but even this was not enough. Castor and Polydeuces had never been separated before and Polydeuces did not wish to live any longer without his twin. His first thought was to kill himself, but this was, of course, impossible. As the son of Zeus he was an immortal, and would simply be taken to live a new life among the gods on Olympus, where his mortal brother could not follow. They would be parted for ever.

Though even Zeus could not change the laws of life and death, with his help a compromise was reached. It was decreed that the twins could spend alternate days together on Olympus and in the Underworld. Each would share the other's world and wherever they were, they would be together.

Jason and the golden fleece

The story of the golden fleece, and of how Jason went with the Argonauts to bring it back to Greece from Colchis on the Black Sea, really begins many years before Jason was born. To find out how the fleece came to be hanging in the branches of a tree in the sacred grove at Colchis, guarded by a creature which was half dragon, half monstrous serpent, we must go back in time to the reign of Bisaltes, king of part of Thrace, and of his daughter, Theophane.

Theophane was very beautiful. In the palace she led a busy domestic life like that of most women of her day, but she liked nothing better than to relax in the sun and swim in the clear waters of the bay near her home. Often she would imagine that she was one of the nereids who lived in the grottos around the rocky shore, and in her imagination she would play with them beneath the waves.

Poseidon, god of the sea, saw her in the water one day. The expression of joy in her dark eyes entranced him, and he carried her off in his chariot to the island of Crumissa, where he hoped to woo her. However, Theophane already had many mortal suitors. Determined to win her back, they sailed after her to the island. Poseidon was annoyed that the suitors should try to thwart his plans, so he turned Theophane into a ewe and when the suitors arrived, they were unable to find her. Naturally they did not think to look among the many flocks of sheep kept by the islanders. They would hardly have recognized Theophane if they had.

It happened that a number of the suitors decided to stay on Crumissa, for they liked the life they found there. Poseidon was therefore unable to change the girl back to her true form, and she continued to live as a ewe among the other sheep. In time she gave birth to a lamb with a fleece of pure gold. On Zeus's orders the lamb was brought back to the mainland of Greece, and was put out to pasture among the flocks which grazed near the citadel of Mycenae on the plain of Argos.

Shortly before this, King Pelops, the ruler of that area, had died, leaving two sons, Atreus and Thyestes. They quarrelled bitterly about which of them should succeed their father on the throne. Many people sided with Atreus, who was the elder, but there were an equal number who supported Thyestes. To avoid the dispute flaring into civil war, the brothers decided to consult the oracle at Delphi.

Atreus and Thyestes travelled north to the great wooded hollow, carved from the face of the mountains, which formed the sacred home

of the great oracle. There they waited for the oracle to speak. Eagles circled over the crags above them and the soft call of a cuckoo drifted to them on the breeze. Silence fell, and at last the voice of the oracle came.

'He amongst whose flocks the lamb with the golden fleece is found shall be the rightful king,' it said.

'A golden lamb? I know of no golden lamb,' Atreus said in puzzlement.

'Nor I,' added Thyestes. 'All we can do is look.'

Apart from the shepherds who looked after the flocks on the plain of Argos, there was one person who knew about the lamb with the golden fleece. This was Atreus's wife Aerope, who had for some while been in love with her husband's brother Thyestes. When the two men returned to Mycenae with the oracle's message, she went secretly at night to move the lamb from the flocks of Atreus to those of Thyestes. When daylight came it was found there and Thyestes became king.

Zeus was not pleased by what had happened. He sent Hermes to Atreus.

'You have been wronged,' Hermes told him. 'You are the rightful king, for the lamb lived under your care and not that of your brother.' Unfortunately, Hermes forgot to mention the part Aerope had played in switching them around.

Atreus told Thyestes what Hermes had said but Thyestes did not believe him. He thought that his brother was simply a bad loser.

'What nonsense is this?' he asked. 'Did we not agree that the oracle should decide? It seems you did not like the answer it gave and now you wish to dispute it.'

'I would accept the decision willingly if I did not suspect that some trickery was involved,' Atreus said, growing angry. He had seen Aerope cast loving glances at Thyestes and suspected he had been the victim of a plot. 'I am as certain that there has been foul play as I am that the sun rises in the east,' he added.

Thyestes laughed scornfully. 'May it rise for one day in the west if you are the true king!' he said.

The quarrel continued through the night. Daybreak came, but it was a strange dawn. Usually the first light came streaming through the window next to where they sat, for it looked out over the eastern hills. However, on this occasion, the courtyard below was in deep shadow. Filled with wonder, they made their way downstairs and into the open air where they could see to the west

across the plain. There the light blinded them, for Helios in his chariot was mounting the sky in the west, far across the distant ocean which lay beyond the Pillars of Hercules. At this unmistakeable sign, Thyestes gave way and Atreus became king in his place. Thyestes was banished forever from the land.

The lamb grew and became a ram, with fine curled horns.

Meanwhile, far to the north at Orchomenos near Thebes another quarrel was developing. Orchomenos was ruled by King Athamas. He had four children, Phrixus and Helle by his first wife, and two others by Ino, his second wife.

Every year Ino grew more and more jealous of her step-children. To her mind, Athamas seemed to favour Phrixus and Helle at the expense of her own children. When she complained about it to the king, he simply laughed at her, for he knew that he treated all four of his children alike. 'You are imagining things,' he told her. 'Stop being so silly!'

This made Ino very angry, though she did not show it. Instead she brooded on her imagined wrongs and thought out a plan to get rid of Phrixus and Helle. She had slow fires lit in cellars beneath the grain stores of the city so that the wheat and barley kept there dried up and became infertile. When it was planted, the grain did not grow: there would soon be famine in the land. Ino then told King Athamas that a messenger had come from the oracle at Delphi saying that if Phrixus and Helle were sacrificed to Zeus all would be well. The corn would sprout, the fields would become green, and a full harvest would be gathered in.

Athamas called together the city council and consulted its members, but he had already made his decision: his two beloved children must die so that all the people of Orchomenos might live. The wise men of the council gave him their sorrowful thanks, and with a heavy heart Athamas gave orders for preparations to be made for the sacrifice.

Zeus, looking down from Olympus, frowned in anger. The sacrifice was to be made in his name, but it had been planned without his approval. Summoning Hermes, he ordered him to fly to Mycenae to fetch the golden ram, which had grown big and strong under the protection of Atreus. Just as the children were being led to the altar, the ram appeared overhead, its fleece shining like the sun. The priests drew back in

terror as a voice came out of the clouds.
'Fly, children! Fly on the ram's back!' cried
Hermes, hovering invisible at the ram's side.
'Fly like the wind over land and sea!'

No one dared to stop Phrixus and Helle as they
scrambled onto the ram's back. Phrixus held fast
to the ram's horns and Helle, sitting behind him,
clung to the curling golden fleece. Then they
were away, circling up into the blue sky before
turning north-east and disappearing from view.

They travelled over many miles of sea. When
they came in sight of land once more, the ram
swooped down. In her excitement, Helle let go of
the fleece with one hand to wave, and lost her
balance. The next moment she was tumbling
down, down, towards the narrow channel of water
which separates Europe from Asia at the western
end of the Sea of Propontis. There she perished,
and to this day the channel is called the Hellespont
in her memory. The ram flew on with Phrixus
across the waters of the Black Sea, landing at
last at Colchis.

Now that the ram's work was done, Zeus
ordered it to be sacrificed, and the golden fleece
from its back was hung from a branch of a tree
in the sacred grove near the palace of King
Aeëtes. There it was guarded by a dragon which
never slept.

At the time of the dispute between Atreus and
Thyestes, Jason, whose name was forever to be

linked with the golden fleece, was growing to
manhood. He lived in a cave on the side of
Mount Pelion with several companions, and was
trained in the arts of hunting and warfare by the
wise old centaur Chiron. Jason's father was
Aeson, the rightful king of Iolchos in Thessaly,
who had been driven from his throne by his half-
brother Pelias. The fugitive king had put Jason
under the care of Chiron to ensure his safety and
because he knew that Chiron would train his son
well for both peace and war.

Chiron had the gift of being able to see into
the future. One day he said to Jason: 'You are
now a man and must go into the world. For you I
see great achievements, but there are many perils
which you must face and overcome first. At times
you will lose heart, but remember always what I
have said and it will give you strength to win
through.'

Jason thanked him and then said: 'I know little
of the ways of the world beyond hunting in the
woods and valleys with you and my friends. Can
you not tell me which way I should go?'
'You might be well advised to visit Iolchos,'
Chiron suggested. 'Who knows but a chance may
come your way to restore your father's kingdom
to him or, if he be dead, to wear the crown
yourself.'

And so, with this firm purpose in view, Jason
set out on his travels.

One day not long afterwards he reached the banks of the river Anaurus. Its muddy waters swirled before him, and as he stood looking at it and wondering how he could cross, he felt a tap on his shoulder. He turned and saw behind him a bent old woman, dressed in rags. She seemed to have appeared from nowhere, for he could have sworn that she had not been on the bank when he reached it. Yet she could only hobble slowly with the aid of a stick, and there was no cover nearby which could have concealed her.

'Good sir,' she croaked, 'Your face is kind. Will you help me to cross the stream?'

'Why,' said Jason, 'I am wondering how I can cross it myself. It looks as though I shall have to wade and, if the water is deep, to swim. If you will risk a ride on my back you are welcome to come with me.'

So he took the old woman on his shoulders and, holding onto the branch of an overhanging tree, lowered himself into the water. The current was strong, but the river was not as deep as he had feared. Nevertheless he had to struggle to reach the farther shore, for as he went the old woman seemed to grow in weight with every step and

the water swirled rapidly, pulling him down. Several times his head was almost submerged, and he had to gasp desperately for air as the spray filled his nostrils. When he finally reached the opposite bank his legs were buckling under him, and having put the old woman safely down, he threw himself on the grass to rest.

It was only then that he noticed that one of his sandals was missing, and with an exclamation of annoyance he bent forward to make sure that the strap of the other one was secure. It was a minute before he looked up. When he did so, there in front of him, in place of the ragged crone, stood a tall, handsome woman. She was dressed in a purple robe, and on her head was a golden crown.

'Do not be afraid, Jason,' she said as he started back, 'and do not grieve at the loss of your sandal in the river. Its loss will be, in the end, your gain, but you must wait a while to see why this should be.'

'Who – who are you?' the young man stammered.

'I am Hera, wife of Zeus and Queen of the Heavens,' the woman said. 'You were kind to an old woman in her hour of need, and did not once

think of throwing her from your shoulders even when you came near to drowning. For this I will watch over you, so go without fear to Iolchos and face the king.' Hera was gone, as quickly and mysteriously as she had come.

Greatly perplexed, Jason journeyed on. When he entered the streets of Iolchos, he noticed that people were looking at him and then turning away, whispering among themselves. This puzzled him and made him feel not a little resentful. He was not a monster with two heads to be stared at and talked about! After a while he took hold of the arm of a passer-by and asked him what was wrong. At first the man was reluctant to answer, but when Jason's strong fingers closed on his arm more tightly, he spoke. 'They say that when a man with one sandal comes, he will depose the king,' he said. Jason remembered Hera's words.

He asked for an audience with King Pelias and noticed that the king's eyes, too, strayed time and again to his bare foot. Clearly he was ill-at-ease, though he seemed friendly enough. 'I expect you think that I have done your father wrong,' the king said. 'Well, that is as may be, but

I am willing to yield the crown to you or to anyone else if they can show themselves more worthy than I am to rule. However, it is not easy to think of a test to find such a man.'

'If he were to bring the golden fleece back from Colchis, I would think him worthy,' said Jason. He was as surprised as the king at his words, for there had been no thought of the magic fleece in his mind before he spoke. He knew little about it, except what he had heard in the tales of the golden ram told round the fire in the evenings he had spent in Chiron's cave.

A look of cunning came into Pelias's eyes. Here was a chance to get rid of the young man, probably for ever. The quest for the fleece would be long and dangerous. It could be a quest from which Jason might well never return.

'If you can get the golden fleece, Iolchos shall be yours,' said Pelias, and the bargain was struck.

Few would have disputed that the task was a great challenge. The journey was likely to be hazardous, so Jason made careful preparations. His ship, the *Argo*, was named after Argus the Thespian, a skilled craftsman who supervised its construction. At Hera's request, Athene sent him a carved prow made from the oaks of Dodona to bring him luck. Argus himself was to sail in the ship, and for the rest of the *Argo*'s crew, Jason called on some fifty of the greatest of the Greek heroes.

First he asked Peleus and Telamon, who had been two of his companions in the days when he lived in Chiron's cave. The mighty Hercules joined them, and as word spread out from Iolchos of the great adventure that was about to start, others came to join Jason. The Dioscuri, Castor and Polydeuces, were two of them. There were also the winged sons of the North Wind, Zetes and Calais and Orpheus, a musician who, though a mortal, rivalled even the god Apollo on the lyre. Though Orpheus was no warrior, he was to play a vital part in the quest for the fleece.

Atalanta, the huntress of Arcadia, was the only woman to join the band of men on the *Argo*; her skill with the bow could match the best of them. Among others who came were Ascalaphus, son of Ares, Echion, son of Hermes, Idmon, son of Apollo, Iphitis, brother of King Eurystheus of Tiryns, and Malempus, son of Poseidon. Together, the crew became known as the Argonauts.

After some weeks they were ready, and early one morning the *Argo* moved smoothly out of the harbour of Iolchos into the calm sea. All Greek boats of that time had both oars and sails, and it was on the oars that Jason relied to take the ship clear of the treacherous rocks and sand banks near the harbour mouth. But once out in the wide Aegean, the white sails were hoisted and the Argonauts made good headway before a stiff breeze. They called briefly at the island of Lemnos and then waited till nightfall to slip unseen, with muffled oars, through the narrow waters of the Hellespont, which King Laomedon of nearby Troy barred to Greek ships.

By morning they were safely through. It was shortly after this that Hercules left them. They had sheltered for a while in a small harbour, and he had gone ashore to cut himself a new oar, for his own had been broken in a rowing match with Jason. When Hercules discovered that the servant who had gone with him was missing, he went in search of him. Neither Hercules nor the servant returned and after several days the Argonauts had to sail without them.

They did this reluctantly, for Hercules was one of the strongest of the heroes, and they knew that a particular peril lay ahead of them. To reach the Black Sea they had to pass through the Bosphorus, a narrow strait between two huge, floating rocks known as the Symphleglades, which clashed together to crush anything which tried to get past them. Just as the rocks towered over their bows, a heron came flying down over the sea ahead of them. As it passed between the rocks, they came together with a sound like thunder, but the heron was a magic bird, sent by Hera, and its flight was faster than the slow beat of its grey wings suggested; it lost only some feathers from its tail.

Slowly the rocks began to part again, and at a

signal from Jason, every oarsman bent his back and the blades dipped. The *Argo* leaped forward under the swift and powerful strokes, moving over the water as if propelled by some magic power. The steep, craggy faces of the rocks loomed on either hand, already drawing together once more. However, the *Argo* passed safely through – though only just, for the ornament at its stern was crushed to pieces.

The Argonauts now swung north, following the eastern coastline of Thrace, until they came to the city of Salmydessus, where King Phineus ruled. Once this king had had the power to see into the future, but he had predicted things which the gods did not wish men to know, and they had blinded him. As an added punishment, they had sent the Harpies to plague him.

The Harpies were loathsome creatures with the bodies and wings of birds, and the heads of ugly women. Whenever Phineus settled to a meal they flew down to snatch the food from his plate before he could eat. Jason promised to help Phineus and a feast was prepared for the Argonauts. King Phineus sat at the head of the table and, as usual, the Harpies swooped down to take the meat that was put before him. The Argonauts were ready for them. Drawing their swords they slashed and stabbed at the clumsy creatures, driving them away again and again. Still they returned, until at last Calais and Zetes, the winged sons of the North Wind, flew up into the air after them and chased them out over the sea, to be seen no more.

In gratitude, Phineus told the Argonauts many things they needed to know if they were to sail safely to Colchis. Then they went on their way. They passed along the coast of the country of the Amazons, where Hercules had taken the girdle of Hippolyte. Near the isle of Ares, the Stymphalian birds suddenly darkened the sky above them. Their brazen feathers rained down on the *Argo*, but following the advice which King Phineus had given them, Jason and his crew protected themselves with their shields and sent a fusillade of arrows up from below, killing many of the birds and driving the marauders away. Fourteen birds fell to Atalanta's bow alone.

And so, at long last, the Argonauts reached the mouth of the river Phasis and rowed the last few miles between its tree-lined banks to the wild, barbarous country of Colchis.

Aeëtes, the king, ruled his subjects harshly. He was a famous magician and what he could not take by force, he took by wizardry. For this reason, his people were always afraid of losing their possessions. He did not welcome the Argonauts' visit and was determined that they should not take the golden fleece. Just the same, he decided that for the moment he would appear friendly. Such an array of fighting strength as that presented by the *Argo*'s crew was not to be dismissed lightly. He would try his magic powers against them first.

'You may have the fleece,' he told Jason, 'but Zeus, by whose agency it was brought to Colchis, decreed that he who takes it must first perform certain tasks.' This was not, of course, true. It was Aeëtes and not Zeus who was making the conditions, though Jason did not know this.

The king went on: 'First you must catch and harness my two fire-breathing, brazen-hooved bulls to a plough, and with it turn the earth of the field of Ares. When this is done, the field must be sown with the dragon's teeth in this bronze helmet here.'

Jason agreed to the king's terms, but their conversation had been overhead by Medea, the

king's daughter. Jason's dark good looks had already won her heart, and she determined to help him, for she knew that no ordinary man could tame the bulls. The fire which came from their flaring nostrils scorched the earth before them for a wide area.

Like her father, Medea had magic powers. From the wild crocus of the mountainside she made an ointment, and on her instructions, Jason smeared himself all over with it. The ointment prevented the fire of the bulls from touching him when he tackled them and he was able to harness them and plough the field. Striding over the newly turned earth, he sowed the dragon's teeth which Aeëtes had given him.

He had scarcely finished when a regiment of fighting men with gleaming breastplates sprang from the ground where the teeth had been sown. The soldiers advanced on the Argonauts with threatening cries. But Medea had advised Jason well. He threw the bronze helmet which had held the teeth among them and at once they turned and began to fight each other. Soon they had all perished.

'You have done well and now the fleece is yours,' Aeëtes told Jason, hiding his anger.

That afternoon, Medea warned Jason that her father planned to send his soldiers to the *Argo* one hour before dawn on the following day to kill them as they slept.
'Before that time, you must have taken the fleece and sailed away,' she told him. 'When night falls I will take you to it, but it would be as well to have someone with us who can play sweet music on the pipes or lyre.'
'Orpheus is with us,' the young man said, puzzled, 'and no one can play the lyre better than he. But why music?'
'That you will see in due course,' Medea told him. 'Make sure Orpheus is with you.'

When night fell Medea saddled three horses and brought them to the quayside where the *Argo* was moored. Jason, Medea and Orpheus mounted and rode through the quiet back streets of the town and out into the countryside. It was a dark night, and without Medea to guide them the winding path over open heathland would have been hard to follow. In the distance, an owl hooted.

On they rode, only the jingle of their horses' harness breaking the silence, until ahead of them, over a low hill, a glow appeared as if a fire burned there. Soon they could see a clump of trees outlined against the dark sky; it was from the middle of these that the mysterious light came.

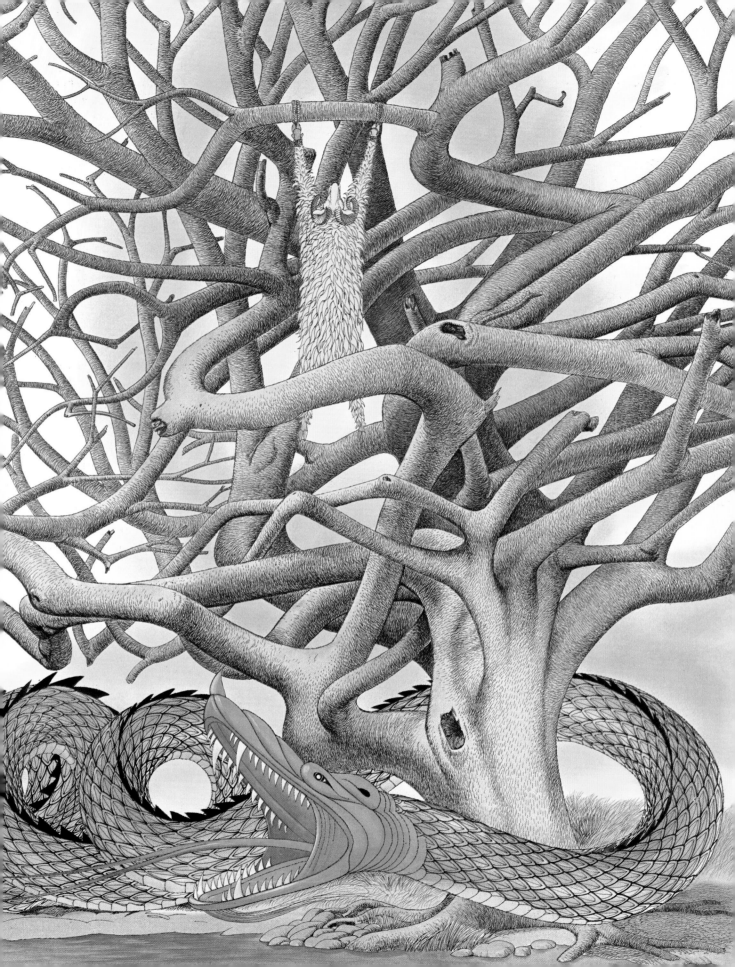

'The sacred grove,' whispered Medea. 'It is the golden fleece that shines like fire.'

They drew nearer cautiously, and presently they could see that what she said was true. High up in the tallest tree of all hung the golden fleece, shedding a white light around it so that the twisted branches threw fantastic shadows out into the surrounding gloom. At the base of the tree, coiled about its trunk, lay the hideous guardian of the fleece, the dragon-serpent about which Jason had heard so much. Its two evil eyes watched them as they moved nearer and Jason drew his sword, prepared to do battle. However, Medea put her hand on his arm.

'Let Orpheus play,' she said.

Wondering again at her words, Jason sheathed his sword and they dismounted. Then Orpheus took the lyre from his back and sat down on a small grassy bank. His fingers plucked at the strings and the notes filled the night air, weaving through the branches of the trees. The music seemed to wrap itself around them as they listened. Gradually, before Jason's astonished gaze, the eyes of the dragon drooped and closed, and soon it slept.

'Now!' said Medea, and Jason advanced into the sacred grove. The dragon did not move. Cautiously he stepped over it and then, with growing confidence, climbed swiftly upwards through the branches of the tree to where the fleece gleamed above him. Clasping it under one arm, he scrambled down once more, and in no time at all the three were on their horses and cantering away while the dragon slumbered on, oblivious of the daring theft that had been carried out.

They reached Colchis some hours before dawn, but they knew that there was no time to lose. Aeëtes's anger would be even greater once he found that the fleece was gone. So they went straight to the *Argo*'s mooring-place, where Medea's young half-brother joined them. Medea had decided to sail with Jason and the Argonauts, and he had chosen to go with her. With muffled oars, the great ship slipped away into the dark water and soon they reached the open sea.

On the first day they made good progress, but early the following morning the lookout at the masthead saw a sail on the horizon behind them. As the strange ship drew nearer, Medea recognized the banner of Aeëtes flying from the rigging. Nearer and nearer it came, speeding over the waves more swiftly than any ordinary ship could go. It was clear that Aeëtes was using his magic power.

But Medea had not been idle. If they had seen what she was doing, it is certain that the Argonauts would have stopped her. A true daughter of her cruel father and of her barbarous homeland, she had lured her half-brother on some pretext into a concealed spot near the stern of the *Argo* and there she had killed him with a dagger. Then she had chopped his body into small pieces and was now dropping them one by one into the sea. By now Aeëtes was close enough to see what she was doing. He gave a command and his own ship slowed so that he could retrieve his dead son's body, piece by piece, as it floated towards him on the waves. Gradually the pursuing ship dropped behind and so, at this terrible price, the Argonauts made good their escape.

Before they reached Greece, the voyagers had to pass close by the islands where the Sirens waited to lure sailors from their ships with magical songs. But Orpheus with his lyre made music more wonderful still and the Argonauts sailed safely by. Only Butes, the youngest among them, was unable to resist the sea maidens, and he plunged into the waves to be with them.

Eventually, without further adventures, the *Argo* arrived at Iolchos. The fleece was dedicated to Zeus and hung in the temple. As Jason now guessed, Zeus and Hera had organized his quest from the beginning, so that the fleece would be returned to Greece. The words which had come to him so mysteriously when he had suggested the journey to Pelias long ago had been not his own but those of a god.

Pelias kept his word and Jason became king in his place. But Medea did not become his queen as she wished. Though she had helped him, he had been so horrified by the way she had treated her half-brother that he now rejected her. She fled to Athens and in due course Jason married Clause, a princess of Corinth.

Jason's adventures were over, but he was not destined to die in peaceful old age. He often wandered to the shore where the *Argo* lay beached and rotting with the passing years. One day while he was standing alone with his memories under the bows, the figurehead, Athene's gift to bring the Argonauts luck, fell on him. There, beside the ship that had brought him both fame and a kingdom, he died alone.

The house of Thebes

Thebes was the principal city of Boeotia, a province which lay to the north of the great city state of Athens. The story of its founding goes back to the time of Cadmus, son of Agenor, the king of Tyre.

Agenor had a beautiful daughter named Europa. One day when she was playing with her companions on the sea shore, a large white bull came towards her. At first she ran away, expecting it to charge and gore her, but the bull was so fine and gentle and looked at her with such wide, calm eyes, that she soon lost her fear and began to stroke its pure white neck. Growing bolder, she made chains of flowers to wind around its horns, and eventually, since it really did seem a peaceful, friendly bull, she clambered onto its broad back.

At once the bull changed; with a snort, it galloped straight towards the edge of the sea and into the waves. As Europa clung terrified to its neck, it swam off in the direction of the island of Crete. When they were safely back on land, the bull vanished as mysteriously as it had appeared. In its place stood the mighty Zeus, explaining that everything he had done had been in the name of love. Europa was soon comforted and in a short time forgot all about her home and family.

Agenor, however, could not forget his beautiful daughter, and he sent his son Cadmus in search of her. He found no sign of her so after some time he travelled to Delphi to ask the oracle of Apollo for advice. This he received, though it was not what he expected. He was told to abandon the search for his sister and instead to follow a cow which he would find in a herd nearby. On the spot where the cow first lay down to rest, he was to found a city.

Everything happened as the oracle had foretold and Cadmus and his men followed the cow for many days, arriving at last in the country called Boeotia. There the cow lay down, and the spot was chosen. Meanwhile, Cadmus's companions had gone to draw water from a nearby well, and discovered that the place was guarded by a fierce, fire-breathing serpent. The serpent killed them all with one searing hot breath, but Cadmus himself, who had stayed to give thanks to the gods, was saved. When his men did not return, he set out to look for them.

After a fierce fight, Cadmus slew the serpent and, on the instructions of the goddess Athene, who appeared at his side, sowed its teeth in the ground. Immediately an army of soldiers sprang up where the strange seed was buried. Cadmus turned to defend himself, but Athene told him to throw a stone amongst them so that they would fight among themselves. The battle was so fierce that only five of the strange soldiers survived; these, known as the Sown Men or Sparti, helped Cadmus to build the Cadmea, the citadel of the city which was to become Thebes. In due course they married and their families played a leading part in the city's history. Cadmus himself married Harmonia, a daughter of Ares, and brought order and civilization to the previously wild country. Legend says that it was Cadmus who taught the Boeotians the use of the alphabet.

Cadmus's life was not an easy one. The serpent he had killed to found the city was, he discovered, sacred to Ares, and the god never really forgave him for destroying it. In his old age he was dethroned by his young grandson and he and his wife Harmonia were cast out of Thebes, to live as best they might in the woods and fields. One weary night, when they had wandered for several days eating only the few berries and roots they could find, Cadmus gave way to despair. 'Since serpents seem so precious to the gods,' he cried, 'I wish I had been born one myself.'

As Harmonia watched, her old husband's body withered and shrunk; mottled scales covered his limbs, and he fell on the ground, coiling his unfamiliar length around her feet.
'If you have any pity, O gods of Olympus, let me join the husband I have followed for so long,' she prayed, and she, too, felt her arms clamped tightly to her sides, as she sank down beside him. Raising their smooth, scaled heads to peer at their new world, the two snakes slid peacefully out of sight under a rock. It is said that from that time, every child in Cadmus's line had the mark of a serpent on its body.

Thebes grew and prospered, much to the annoyance of its powerful neighbour, Athens. There was constant rivalry between the two cities. Thebes strengthened its position as capital of Boeotia by forming a confederacy of all the chief towns in the area. At meetings of a joint council, each town had a say in the way Boeotian affairs were run, and each town, except one, contributed its share of fighting men to a united army. The exception was Plataea, which refused to join the confederacy and sided with Athens, increasing the bitterness between the two capitals. During the Peloponnesian war, which was fought between a number of the Greek states, the Athenian army was defeated. Later Thebes overcame Sparta, its chief remaining rival, and for a while ruled over a large part of Greece.

The greatest family in Thebes after the time of Cadmus was that of the Labdacids, who were descended from the daughter of one of the Sown Men. However, now and again the line would be broken for a while and a usurper would rule. One such was King Laius, who was warned by an oracle that he would die by the hand of his own son. When a son was born to his wife, he had the child taken to Mount Cithaeron and left there to die, his feet pierced with a spike and bound with cord.

Mount Cithaeron lies in the part of Boeotia nearest to Corinth. The child was found by shepherds of the Corinthian king, Polybus, who had always wished for a son but who had none of his own. The shepherds took the baby to court and told their story, and he was brought up as if he were Polybus's own child. The name given to him was Oedipus, which meant 'swollen foot', for the spike and the tightly-bound cords that bound his feet when he was found had left their mark.

Though Oedipus was raised as the king's son, he was teased cruelly by his young companions because he did not know who his true father was. At first this did not worry him too much, but by the time he grew up, his desire to find out the answer to the riddle of his origin had grown strong. At length he decided to go to Delphi to consult the oracle. He was to regret bitterly that he had done so, for at the sacred shrine he learned that his fate was to kill his father and to marry his own mother. The oracle would tell him neither where they could be found nor who they might be.

The young man was filled with horror at the oracle's disclosures and he resolved never to return to Corinth. King Polybus and his wife Periboea might or might not be his true parents, but they were the only ones he had ever known, and he could not risk harming them. Instead he decided to journey to Thebes to seek his fortune there.

He had travelled a considerable distance and, with only about one day's journey to go, was walking in a narrow valley when he noticed in the distance a chariot approaching. As it drew closer, he could see from the charioteer's fine clothes and the rich trappings of his horses that he must be of noble birth. He was accompanied by two armed men.

The chariot rapidly drew level. When Oedipus did not at once step onto the bank at the side of

the road to let it pass, the charioteer, raising his whip, shouted at him to get out of the way.

'I stand aside for no man who is so impolite,' Oedipus told him.

'Insolent dog!' shouted the stranger, his face darkening with anger. He gestured to the two soldiers. 'Deal with this wretch' he commanded.

The two men sprang forward, drawing their swords, but Oedipus had learned swordsmanship in the royal school of Corinth and they were no match for him. In minutes they lay on the ground, mortally wounded.

'Now, sir,' said Oedipus, addressing the strange nobleman, who had watched the fight from his chariot, 'two against one was uneven odds. One against one should be a fairer fight. Let us see what your sword can do, and whether it matches your tongue for sharpness.' He rushed forward and lunged with his own sword as he spoke.

The charioteer half parried the thrust, but at the noise of the swords clashing so close to them, the chariot horses took fright. They reared up so that the stranger was thrown sideways onto the sword point before Oedipus could withdraw it, and with a cry the man slumped forward, dead.

Oedipus rested a while and then went on, relieved that his instructors in the art of war had taught him so well. But there was one thing that he did not know. The noble charioteer had been none other than his own father, King Laius of Thebes. The first part of the prophecy of the Delphic oracle had come true.

Within a short distance of Thebes stood Mount Phicium, and on it, overlooking the road, the Sphinx had made its home. The Sphinx had a lion's body and an eagle's wings but her head was that of a woman. She had been sent to harass travellers journeying to and from the city in

99

order to punish King Laius for a misdeed. She would ask each passer-by a riddle – to which none had so far found the right answer. When they failed, she would fly at them, laughing horribly, and strangle them with her clawed hands.

Few people now ventured along the road for none of those who had done so had returned. Only by taking a little-known path, which avoided Mount Phicium by going up into the mountains, had Laius and his men escaped the Sphinx's clutches. Now, as Oedipus approached, he saw the hideous shape crouching by the roadside. The Sphinx saw him too and strode across his path, spreading her wings to make it impossible for him to pass. Beneath heavy brows her eyes glinted wickedly.

'Stay!' she commanded. 'Only if you can answer this riddle will you reach the city. If you fail, you shall die!'

'In that case,' said Oedipus, 'I had better try.'

'What being is it,' asked the Sphinx, 'that at one time in its life goes on four legs, at another on two, and yet when it is old has three?'

Oedipus did not even hesitate. 'Why, man,' he said. 'As a baby he crawls on four legs and then, when he is grown up, he walks on two. In old age a walking stick becomes the third leg.'

The Sphinx's eyes blazed with anger. She danced and screamed with rage, for now the answer to the riddle had been given she was powerless to do further harm. Then she turned and, flapping her wings she half ran, half flew high up onto the mountain, to cast herself down from a high cliff onto the rocks below. Oedipus went on into the city, where the people greeted him as their deliverer.

Shortly after he arrived news came that King Laius's body had been found. It was thought that he had been killed by robbers and a search for the culprits began. Oedipus did not connect the king's death with his own encounter with the charioteer and when the Thebans offered him the vacant throne in gratitude for what he had done, he accepted. Laius's wife, Jocasta became his queen. Without knowing it, Oedipus had married his own mother, and thus the second part of the prophecy of the oracle was fulfilled.

A terrible plague settled on the land. People died of the strange fever in their thousands, and Thebes became a place of mourning. Once more the Delphic oracle was consulted, and this time it said: 'The plague will not be lifted from the land until the murderer of King Laius is banished from among you.'

Surprised and angered that it was someone from Thebes itself who had murdered the king, Oedipus intensified the search for the robbers who had attacked Laius. Still they could not be found. Then one day Teiresias, a blind old man and a renowned soothsayer, came to the court and asked for an audience. In deference to a man so widely respected for his wisdom, Oedipus saw him without delay, and the blind man said that he alone had the answer to the city's problems and could remove the plague.

'Continue', Oedipus said. 'If you can indeed save Thebes, tell me how.'

Teiresias took some time to come to the point for he rambled in his speech, but gradually, Oedipus began to pick up the threads of a story which he thought was known to him alone, for it was the story of his own life. His heart grew heavy as he listened, and everything that had puzzled him about his birth and his more recent life in Thebes became clear. If what the old man said was true, it was he who had murdered Laius, his own father, and his mother Jocasta had become his wife.

Confirmation of the soothsayer's terrible story was soon obtained from Corinth and Jocasta, unable to bear the shame of incest, killed herself. Oedipus realized that, even after the plague was lifted, he could no longer remain king of Thebes. He accepted banishment willingly. Then, alone and friendless, he wandered away into the hills, where he blinded himself in penance for the misfortune he had, without knowing it, brought to others.

After Oedipus had gone, twin brothers were chosen to rule Thebes alternately: Polynices for one year, Eteocles for the next. It was hardly an arrangement which could be expected to work well, and the character of one twin, Eteocles, doomed it to failure. At the end of his first year of rule he refused to give up the crown and turned his brother out of the city.

Polynices fled to the court of Adrastus, king of Argos, furious at his brother's action. He rallied six famous warriors and their armies to his aid. First there was Adrastus himself and his son-in-law Tydeus of Calydon, who bore a grudge against Eteocles. They were followed by Adrastus's brother-in-law Amphiaraus, who was unwilling to join the others, for he felt that they were bound to fail. He could see into the future, and a

she did so she left the small boy who was in her charge on his own. She waited with them while the men drank and filled their pitchers. When they returned to the road they were horrified to see the child lying dead, with a serpent coiled about its legs. The men killed the serpent and were about to move on when Amphiaraus held up his hand and spoke.

'This is an evil omen for a venture which has been ill-starred from the beginning,' he said. 'We must honour the boy or every chance of success will be gone.'

His words could not be ignored, so the army camped by the pool for several days. They held funeral games in the boy's honour and celebrated all the rites which would give the boy's soul a safe passage to the Underworld. Then, rested and refreshed, the soldiers took up their arms and once more marched on to Thebes.

On the plain under the shadow of Mount Phicium, where Oedipus had outwitted the Sphinx, the army halted. Polynices sent Tydeus into the city to demand its surrender. Eteocles rejected the idea without even considering it, so Tydeus challenged some of the best Theban warriors to single combat. He defeated so many that no more dared to come forward. Then he returned to Polynices with Eteocles's reply. The attacking armies were deployed, one before each of the seven gates.

Meanwhile the blind seer of Thebes, Teiresias, asked for an audience with Eteocles.

'The situation is grave,' he said, 'and we will only be victors if the son of one of our noble families will sacrifice himself to Ares, god of war.' There were many volunteers who offered to give their lives, but it was a young noble, Menoeceus, who threw himself to his death from the battlements. The Thebans gained courage from his brave action. They repulsed the first attack and killed Capaneus: the first of the seven was lost. In a counter-attack Hippomedon and Parthenopaeus also fell to the Theban fighting men and the gallant Tydeus was so badly wounded that he could no longer play an active part.

Of the seven, only Polynices, Adrastus and Amphiaraus now remained. After the last skirmish Eteocles and his soldiers had retired into the city, but on the battlefield many hundreds of men of both sides lay dead. The sight sickened Polynices, and he decided that only he could save further slaughter. He strode from the ranks of his

picture had formed in his mind of the seven of them lying dead in the dust before the gates of Thebes. However, his wife was offered as a bribe a fine gold necklace, which had once belonged to Cadmus's wife, and she persuaded him to change his mind.

Parthenopaeus, the son of the huntress Atalanta, was an old ally of Adrastus, and he, with Capaneus and Hippomedon, made up the seven. When they were assembled, Polynices held a council of war.

'First I would like to thank you for coming to my aid,' he said. 'It is a worthy cause. My brother has shown that he cannot be trusted as a ruler should be, if he is to have the respect of his subjects.' The others murmured their agreement and Polynices went on: 'It is not by chance that I have asked six of you to join me. There are seven gates to the city of Thebes, and we have seven leaders. Adrastus has divided his army into two, one half for himself and one for me, so we have seven armies. Each will attack one gate, and we will take the place by storm.'

And so the seven armies, marching for the time being as one, set out for Thebes, with Polynices and Adrastus at the head. On the way they halted for a while in Nemea, near where they had heard that there was a pool of fresh water, for they needed to replenish their supplies. A servant-girl offered to show them where the pool was. While

men and stood alone before the city walls.
'Brother Eteocles!' he called in a ringing voice.
'Enough men have died in the quarrel between
us. Will you come, unguarded by your men, to
fight with me and so make a final settlement of
our differences?'

Eteocles was not a cowardly man and his
voice came back from the highest point of the
citadel, where he had watched his twin advance
alone.
'I accept!' he cried, and a cheer rose from the
ranks of both sides. Then the noise died away
and the warriors watched in total silence as the
gates of Thebes were thrown open and Eteocles,
his helmet gleaming in the sun and his sword at
the ready came striding out of the city.

The two brothers faced each other for a
moment. Neither spoke. The only sound came
from a banner fluttering on the city walls.
Polynices made the first move, darting forward,
but Eteocles diverted his blade deftly with his
shield and aimed a counter-blow which Polynices
warded off with equal skill. Slowly the brothers
circled round, fighting like the champions they
were, but it began to seem that they were too
evenly matched for either to gain advantage over
the other. Still the soldiers watched in silence
from the plain and from along the walls of
Thebes, ready to cheer the victor if he proved to
be on their side.

Then, unexpectedly and with great swiftness,
the end came. Both lunged at the same moment
with their swords, letting their guards fall and
relying only on the swiftness of the move to see
them safely through. Each had had the same plan
of action in mind and each wounded the other
mortally. Together they fell dying.

For a moment the onlookers remained silent,
too stunned to move, but then a sharp word of
command rang out from the open gateway. The
Theban noble Creon had seen his leader fall and
taken swift command. The men of Thebes,
chanting wild war-cries, poured from the seven
gates, and almost at once Polynices's army fled
before them in hopeless disarray. Of the seven
leaders, only Adrastus, King of Argos, managed
to escape.

Creon, the new leader of the Thebans, dispensed
savage justice and would not allow burial of the
defeated men.
'Let them rot where they lie and may the vultures
pick their bones!' he said, contemptuously. 'Why
should we honour them by burial?'

But Antigone, sister of Polynices and Eteocles,
was determined that Polynices at least should not
be left lying in the sun. She summoned those of
her servants whom she could trust, the ones who
had served the family well and happily for many
years before Polynices's banishment. She knew
that they would be loyal to his memory, and she
led them out onto the plain under cover of night
to steal the body away. On the lower slopes of
Mount Phicium they dug a grave by the light of
torches, and lowered Polynices reverently into it.
The next night masons went out with her to
build a tomb over the grave.

When morning came and Creon looked out
from the citadel, he saw that the body of
Polynices was gone. He sent out searchers and
they found Antigone standing alone beside the
tomb, thinking of the happier days when she and
her two brothers had played together as children
on that very mountain.

When Creon heard what Antigone had done,
he ordered his son Haemon to take a party of
men and to wall up Antigone in Polynices's
tomb. She would swiftly learn that his orders
were to be obeyed, and she would serve as a
warning to others who might decided to bury
their dead in secret. Haemon pretended to agree
to carry out his father's wishes, but Antigone was
the girl whom he had chosen to be his wife.
Instead of taking men with him to the mountain,
he went alone on a fast horse and carried her
away to a safe place where they could be married
and live together without the new king hearing
of it.

Meanwhile Adrastus had returned to Argos, and
news soon reached him of Creon's harsh ruling.
In those times it was considered barbarous not to
honour a foe who had fought well and been
fairly defeated in battle, by giving him proper
burial. However, Adrastus's own army was in a
poor state and it was useless to attempt to fight
again so soon. Instead, he set out for Athens,
where he knew he would have a sympathetic
hearing, for Athens and Thebes were old enemies.

Theseus, king of Athens at that time, gladly
accepted this chance for his armies to march
against his hated neighbour. The Athenians took
Thebes completely by surprise and overran it
without difficulty. Creon was imprisoned, but
was first made to watch as a great funeral pyre
was lit on the plain of Thebes and the dead
warriors of Polynices's armies were given burial
rites that would ensure their peaceful afterlife.

Theseus, king of Athens

Theseus, one of the greatest of the Greek heroes, was born in Troezen, a city lying on a flat plain bordering the sea. His mother, Aethra, was the king of Troezen's daughter; his father was Aegeus, king of the great city state of Athens.

Some time before Theseus was born, Aegeus left Troezen and his young wife to return to Athens alone. Athens was many weeks' journey away and it was uncertain when, if ever, Aegeus would return. Before he left, he took Aethra and six strong men outside the gates of the city to a place where a great rock towered up from the plain, close by a clump of pines.

'Our first-born will be a son, and he shall be called Theseus,' Aegeus told them. 'When he is a man he will journey to see me, and I will leave a token here which he must bring with him and by which I will know him.' He took off his sandals and put his sword beside them on the ground.

'These I will place beneath the rock,' he said. 'When Theseus grows to manhood he will have the strength of an ox, so that he can cast the rock aside. Carrying the sword and wearing the sandals he will come to Athens, and when I see them I will know that he really is my son.'

The six strong men positioned the beam of wood under one side of the rock and, with their combined strength, tilted it so that the sword and sandals could be placed underneath. The rock was lowered gently into place again. Then Aegeus set out on his journey and in due course the son was born.

The years passed and Theseus grew to manhood, handsome, strong, a great athlete and well trained in the arts of combat. Aegeus did not return and Theseus told Aethra: 'I must journey to see my father, and take my rightful place as son of the King of Athens.'

Aethra was sorry to let him go, but she knew that he was determined. She took him to the place of the great rock, for she had told him of his father's words many times, and he knew what he had to do.

The young man bent down beside the rock and the muscles of his shoulders and arms rippled under his skin, bronzed by the hot summer's sun. He needed no beam as a lever, for his strength was like the strength of an ox, and the rock toppled to one side as if it were no more than a pebble. Sheathing the sword and putting on the sandals, Theseus bade farewell to his mother and strode off southwards across the plain towards the distant hills. His journey had begun.

Theseus had chosen to take the land route to Athens, a way that he knew held many perils, for bandits and monsters roamed the countryside. He fought with and vanquished a number of these, until one day he arrived in a valley where the people lived in terror of an evil giant of a man named Sinis. The shepherds no longer dared to take their flocks of sheep and goats to graze on the hillsides where Sinis lived alone in a cave. No one was safe from him, and whoever he captured he killed. His favourite method was to bend two strong pine saplings to the ground and tie his victims to them. With a great shout of laughter, he would release the saplings and the luckless peasants would be torn apart.

'Help us,' the peasants pleaded, 'for word has already reached us that you are a great and fearless warrior.' So Theseus wrestled with Sinis and, when he had overcome him, he tied him to his own saplings to be torn apart like his victims. Theseus journeyed on and soon came to a place where the road from Megara to Athens ran beside the sea. After a while it wound upwards along the face of a tall cliff, a narrow, perilous place, with a sheer drop to the rocks and the foaming sea far below. At its highest point, where the wind whistled and moaned in tune with the wild cry of the gulls wheeling there, a huge figure suddenly strode out from a cleft in the rock and barred his path.

'Bow down before the mighty Sciron!' the man demanded, and his voice echoed like a roll of thunder, back from the rocks. 'None shall pass this way until I give him leave and a tribute has been paid. Each traveller along this road must humble himself before me. If he will not kneel and wash my feet he goes no further.'

Theseus stood his ground. 'I pay homage to no man who has not the skill to defeat me in combat,' he said quietly. 'Only then will I acknowledge him master.' He strode forward as if to pass.

Sciron rose to his full height and Theseus drew his sword. For a moment they stood there on the narrow ledge, eyeing each other warily. Sciron carried no weapons, but he was obviously immensely strong and he towered over Theseus.

The young Athenian lunged with his sword and Sciron retreated a little, weaving sideways from the thrust. Theseus followed, perilously near to the edge of the cliff, and as he did so he noticed a cunning gleam in Sciron's eyes, which glowed like coals beneath his heavy brows. Prepared for almost any trick, Theseus waited, but perhaps

only he could have countered the move which came next.

Suddenly Sciron threw himself backwards to the ground, and as he did so he kicked out viciously at Theseus's legs, intending to unbalance him and send him toppling from the ledge. This move was so unexpected that only a great athlete like Theseus could have survived. With the quickness of a panther he leaped sideways and with his right hand caught Sciron's ankle in a grip like bands of steel. Gathering his strength, he pulled with all the power he possessed and, twisting his body, hurled the giant right over the edge of the cliff.

After resting for a while Theseus went on to the next village. The people there were rejoicing, dancing in the streets, for they had heard the terrible cry that had come from Sciron's throat as he fell to his death. For many years travellers had been forced by the giant guardian of the road to kneel and wash his feet. Even then they did not escape, for as they knelt, Sciron would kick them from the cliffs so that they fell to the rocks below. It was a long time now since anyone had dared to go that way.

Theseus had not gone many miles when Cercyon the Arcadian stepped out into the road in front of him. This was a giant of a man and a great wrestler. He used to challenge everyone who came past his home and was so strong that he

would crush to death those who were rash enough to oppose him. So far his strength alone had served him well, but he did not know that he was now face to face with a man who had studied wrestling as an art. It was Theseus who first realized that quick thinking and agility would always overcome brute force.

Theseus accepted the challenge and a fight was arranged. Demeter, Zeus's sister, was among the watchers. The two men circled round each other but when the lumbering Cercyon made a move to seize Theseus, somehow Theseus was no longer there. Baffled, the giant whirled round and as he did so he felt his legs pinioned. Next moment, arms flailing wildly, he was lifted bodily into the air, and Theseus had dashed him to the ground with such force that death was instantaneous. Skill had outwitted strength.

Theseus had one more battle to fight before his journey came to an end. This was against Procrustes, an apparently friendly bandit, who offered hospitality to pilgrims travelling to worship at the shrine of Demeter at Eleusis. Procrustes would welcome the weary pilgrims to his cave home with wine and feasting and then show them to a bed which he had prepared for them. Grateful for a comfortable night's rest, they would lie down – and Procrustes would suddenly change from his role of smiling host. If the traveller was too tall for the bed, with one

blow of his sword he would cut off his legs; if he was too short for it, Procrustes would order the members of his band to stretch the victim on a rack until he fitted the length of the bed exactly.

Procrustes entertained Theseus with his usual good humour and when at last the Athenian lay down on the bed, he drew his sword, for Theseus was too tall for it by far. But Procrustes was slow and clumsy in his movements and Theseus had learned something about tricks from his encounter with Sciron; he kicked out violently at the hand which held the sword. Procrustes cried out in pain and the sword flew from his hand across the room as Theseus leaped on him like a tiger and strangled him with his bare hands. The other bandits, who had been waiting outside, were so terrified by this show of prodigious strength that they cowered back into the shadows of the rocks around the cave and did not trouble Theseus any further.

And so Theseus drew near to Athens. Even there his problems were not entirely over. Medea, abandoned by Jason at Corinth, had since sought refuge in Athens with her young son, Medus. A woman of strange fancies, she feared that Theseus would usurp the place of favour at the royal court which she hoped for Medus. She arranged to be the first to welcome the young traveller, meeting him in an antechamber of the palace before anyone else knew of his arrival. On her

instructions, her servants offered Theseus a draught of refreshing wine into which, unknown to any but herself, she had dropped a deadly poison.

Theseus was raising the goblet to his lips when there was the sound of footsteps from an inner court, and the great wooden doors at the end of the chamber were thrown wide. In the opening stood the majestic figure of Aegeus, and Medea, terrified of discovery, dashed the goblet from Theseus's hand. With one glance, Aegeus recognized the sword and sandals which he had left so long ago under the great rock of Troezen. He embraced Theseus, and there was great feasting and rejoicing in Athens for many days.

However, Aegeus had also seen the look in Medea's eyes and he guessed what had been in her mind, for he knew of her dangerous, jealous passions. She and her son Medus were driven from the city and forced to flee back to the kingdom of her father at Colchis, where she had first met and loved Jason.

At the time of Theseus's return to Athens a cousin of his named Daedalus was living there. The other sons of the Athenian princes were warriors and hunters. They were admired for their skill with the bow and spear and for their physical strength, but Daedalus cared little for these things and was instead a lover of the arts, already known as a great sculptor and architect. He was a master of many crafts. He not only designed beautiful buildings and carved fine statues, but he also invented many of the tools and instruments used to create them. His was the first axe for hewing wood and the first chisel for shaping it, and he turned his skill to many other things as well. He was the first to make masts and sails for ships which, until that time, had depended only on the strength and stamina of many oarsmen.

Daedalus had large workshops in Athens, where other men worked under his supervision. One of his many apprentices was his nephew Talus, a young boy who showed promise of a skill to rival even that of his uncle. Daedalus was not used to competition. At first he was simply jealous and found fault constantly instead of giving advice and encouragement, but when Talus also began to match him in the invention of tools to help to improve their work, he became thoroughly angry. It was Talus who made the first potter's wheel and used the backbone of a fish as the first primitive woodsaw.

At that time Talus and his uncle were working in the Acropolis, which stands on a hill above the city of Athens, flat-topped, but with steep cliffs along its edge. What happened was never really discovered, but one evening Talus vanished and was never seen again. Daedalus, whose envy of his nephew was known, was accused of pushing him over the cliffs onto the boulder strewn slopes at their base.
'He fell, but by accident,' Daedalus explained, 'and as he fell the great goddess Athene took pity. She turned him into a partridge – you know he is often called by that name – and he flew off towards the woods on the Hill of Ares.' Talus was also known as Perdix which, in Greek, does indeed mean partridge.

Certainly the body of Talus was never found, which seemed to bear out what Daedalus had said, but his story was none-the-less greeted with scepticism. He was summoned to the Court of Areopagus, which traditionally sat in judgement on the summit of the Hill of Ares, facing the Acropolis across the valley. Not as skilled in argument as he

was with his hands, Daedalus failed to convince the court, and he was banished from Athens for all time.

He set sail soon after with his son Icarus, making for the city of Knossos in the island kingdom of Crete. There King Minos welcomed him, for Daedalus's fame as a builder and craftsman had long been known beyond the mainland of Greece. Soon he was established in new workshops and was designing buildings of great magnificence for the Cretan king.

Fine as they all were, none of the buildings was more admired nor achieved such fame as the Labyrinth of Knossos, a huge maze with high walls, covering several acres of ground. So complicated was it in design that no one but Daedalus could find his way through its twisting passages. It was built to house the fearsome Minotaur, a creature born of the union of Parsiphaneä and a white bull, a monster half man and half bull itself. Ringed by a hedge of thorns, it lived in the very centre of the Labyrinth, existing only on human flesh. It was said that no man could survive the onslaught of its scythe-like horns.

Each year, seven youths and seven maidens from cities dominated by the Cretan king were sacrificed to it to appease its hunger. Athens had to pay this terrible tribute every ninth year, and the time came soon after young Theseus had returned to the capital. He offered to be one of the seven youths – to give his life if necessary, though he was determined to sell it dearly.

The ship which carried the victims to Crete was always rigged with the black sails of sorrow both on its outward journey and on its tragic return. Theseus, however, was confident that he would return triumphant.
'If I am successful,' he said to Aegeus, 'my ship will have white sails as I come home. You will be able to see them from far off and they will tell you that the news is good. I'll expect you to have a fine feast ready for us all by the time we reach the shore.'
'And if the news is bad?'
'It won't happen,' said Theseus, 'but black of course is the colour of sorrow and despair.'

So Theseus and his companions set sail. When they landed in Crete his good looks and fine bearing won the heart of Ariadne, the daughter of King Minos, and she resolved that he should not die. She knew that Theseus was a cousin of Daedalus, and she went straight to him for help. But Daedalus was afraid.

'I have been banished unjustly from my homeland,' he said. 'Why should I now risk the anger of the king who has befriended me?'

But Ariadne pleaded. 'My father need never know that I came to see you,' she pointed out, and Daedalus began to hesitate. He was, after all, an Athenian himself. Finally he said:
'All right, I will help you, but you must never, never, tell a single person, even at the day of your death. Do you swear to that?'

Ariadne nodded. 'I swear it by all the gods,' she said solemnly.

So Daedalus told her that, fierce as the Minotaur was, it could be vanquished by a man brave enough to stand and fight; most people were overcome by its hideous appearance and evil reputation before they even attempted to attack it. It could be slain only if its brain was pierced by one of its own horns, though how this was to be achieved the unwarlike Daedalus could not say. Finding a way out of the maze was almost as great a problem as killing the monster, but to this Daedalus knew the answer. He gave Ariadne a ball of silken cord with which Theseus would be able to find his way through the Labyrinth. If she tied one end of the cord to the lintel of the maze doorway, the ball would unwind itself, threading its way through the twists and turns of the passages to the spot at the very centre where the Minotaur waited for its prey. Theseus had only to follow the silken cord to go directly to the monster's lair. If he survived the fight, the thread would lead him safely back to the world outside.

Early on the day the tribute of human life had to be paid, Ariadne went with Theseus and his companions to the doorway of the Labyrinth. Just inside they paused and Ariadne tied one end of the cord securely to the lintel. She put the ball on the ground and it rolled away into the maze, just as Daedalus had predicted.
'Wait for me here,' Theseus said, keeping his voice low so that the guards outside should not hear. 'This is a task for me alone. If I should not return within an hour, you will know that I have failed you. Then you must save yourselves as best you can. May the gods protect us.'

Purposefully he strode away, following the line of the silken cord, his sandals making no sound on the soft earth floor. Soon the curved walls of the passages hid him from view. Silently and with anxious faces the others waited in the shadows beside the doorway.

Round corner after corner, this way and that, the cord wound its way in a seemingly endless line. The high walls pressed in on him and the thin strip of sky seemed very far above. After a time Theseus guessed that the centre of the Labyrinth must be drawing near, for he could hear a stamping of hooves ahead of him which made the very earth tremble. More cautiously now he went on, drawing his sword as he did so. Even though he knew that it could not kill the Minotaur, he thought that he might be able to inflict a wound which would weaken it for the final struggle. It gave him confidence to have his familiar sword at the ready.

At last ahead of him the walls of the passage suddenly opened out into a wide circle, with a hedge of vicious briars making another ring within it. All was now still, silent as the night. Theseus stood there, tensed and waiting, unwilling to make any move until he knew just how and from where the attack would come. He sensed that from somewhere behind the thorny hedge two evil eyes were watching him and waiting, too.

Then all at once there came a mighty roar as the Minotaur burst from the thicket. Head down it charged, but Theseus stood like a rock in its path. The horns of the monster flashed in the morning sunlight, more deadly than any spear

and with the full weight of the Minotaur's huge body behind them; but Theseus was ready.

Just as it seemed that nothing could save him, he dropped sideways, threw his sword away and grasped one of the Minotaur's deadly horns in a wrestler's grip. He twisted, throwing his whole weight forwards, and there came a crack like the branch of an oak wrenched from its tree in a winter gale as the horn was torn from its socket. With a bellow of rage, the Minotaur turned and charged again, but before it could gather speed Theseus, using the horn like a javelin, thrust forward with all his might. With a terrible cry, the monster fell, mortally wounded by the weapon with which it had itself destroyed so many.

A swift escape from Crete was now vital, before King Minos discovered how he had been tricked and Theseus hastily followed the cord back to where the others waited. The guards, considering their duty well done now that the prisoners were inside the maze, were dozing at their posts and it was too early in the morning for the rest of the city to be awake. The Athenians crept stealthily to the harbour where their ship was waiting, slipped anchor and sailed away, taking Ariadne with them.

It was only a matter of time before King Minos learned what had happened. The death of the monster was in some ways a relief, but the loss of his prisoners and his beloved daughter was a deadly insult. As Daedalus had feared, he realized at once that there was only one person who could have helped Theseus – the maze-builder himself. Though Minos was angry, he still wanted Daedalus to work for him and he imprisoned him with his son Icarus in the centre of the Labyrinth. All the tools of his workshop were moved there but the entrance gates were heavily guarded by soldiers, so there seemed no hope of escape. Nor would there have been for any ordinary man. Daedalus, however, had a plan.

He made himself a strong bow of an ash wand and a leather thong, and with it he shot two eagles which circled against the white clouds overhead. He plucked them and made wings for himself and his son, arranging the feathers carefully so that they overlapped on a light framework. They were secured at their bases with strong wax, which quickly hardened to hold them in place. The framework of each wing could be strapped to the arms.

'Now we can fly as though we, ourselves, were eagles,' Daedalus said. 'But we must wait until

morning, until just before the guards of the Labyrinth are changed. They will be weary after their long vigil through the night, and will not be so alert.'

And so, not long after the sun rose from the sea in the east on the following morning, Daedalus and Icarus strapped on their wings and soared into the air above the Labyrinth. Drowsing at their posts, King Minos's soldiers did not see them until too late. Frantically they drew their bows, and their arrows sang through the cold morning air, but by that time Daedalus and his son were too high for them to reach and the arrows dropped harmlessly amongst the rocks of the surrounding hillside.

Daedalus and Icarus flew north for some while, towards the islands of the Aegean Sea, on one of which they could rest if they grew weary. 'The sun is climbing fast in the sky,' Daedalus told his son. 'Soon it will have the full heat of the day, so do not fly too high or it will melt the wax which holds the feathers in your wings.'

For an hour or so Icarus obeyed his father, but as his wings swept the air, he thrilled at the power of them. He felt that he was now an eagle, a true king of the air. What the birds could do, so could he. So he began to climb and paid no heed to his father's desperate cries of warning. Up and up he went, into the eye of the sun. The light grew brighter, the air around became hot and Daedalus was soon far below him.

Presently one feather from Icarus's wings floated down, but he did not notice it. Then another and then a third. Too late he realized that his father's warning was coming true. The wax was melting fast and now whole bunches of feathers were drifting backwards behind him. Daedalus turned back to try to help, but by then Icarus was falling, as his wings would no longer support him. Down and down he went, faster and faster, while Daedalus circled helplessly, quite unable to break his headlong fall. With one last cry, Icarus perished in the sea which since that day has borne his name, the Icarian Sea.

Daedalus flew wearily onwards, resting for a while on the islands as he went. He reached Greece, but was still not welcome there, and he knew, too, that the vengeful King Minos might come to Athens seeking him. Eventually he set sail for Sicily and over the years wandered restlessly further and further west in the Mediterranean Sea. No one really knows where he ended his days and whether he died in poverty.

Theseus and Ariadne sailed away from Crete happily. Theseus had not only freed his people from the threat of the Minotaur, he now also found that he loved Ariadne as she loved him. They spent many happy days planning their lives together, and the great alliance that would eventually grow between their kingdoms. But one night as Theseus lay asleep on the deck he had a dream which turned his joy to sadness. In the dream he learned that Ariadne was destined to be the wife of the god Dionysus, and could never marry him. In those days, such dreams were taken as true prophecies and even before he awoke, Theseus knew that he could not go against the fates, however much sorrow it caused him.

The ship called shortly afterwards at the island of Naxos, and the whole company went ashore. Early the next morning Theseus, broken-hearted, sailed away, leaving Ariadne asleep and unsuspecting on the beach. As the dream had foretold, Dionysus later claimed her as his bride.

The ship now drew near to the coast of Greece where day after day King Aegeus waited, looking out over the southern seas from high up on the Acropolis, watching for the flutter of white sails that would tell him his son was still alive. Theseus, however, was thinking only of Ariadne and had completely forgotten the promise he had made. Black sails carried his ship over the blue water towards Athens. Aegeus was the first to see them sailing over the horizon and, overcome with sorrow, he drowned himself before the first messengers arrived with the good news. So, by mischance, Theseus became king of Athens.

Theseus ruled over Athens for many years and was a good and wise king. His armies fought off an invasion of the Amazons and their queen, Hippolyte, became his wife. He was a friend of Hercules and gave him shelter after he had been tricked into killing his own wife, Megara, and his three sons. It is even said that he descended into Hades to help his friend Pirithous to carry off Persephone, and was imprisoned there until Hercules rescued him.

At long last the ageing Theseus was driven from Athens by rebellion and fled to the island of Skyros, where some say he was murdered. However, there is a fitting end to his story, for after the Persian wars an oracle told of the bones of a gigantic man buried on Skyros. His sword and sandals told searchers that this was Theseus, and his remains were brought home and buried in the Athens he loved.

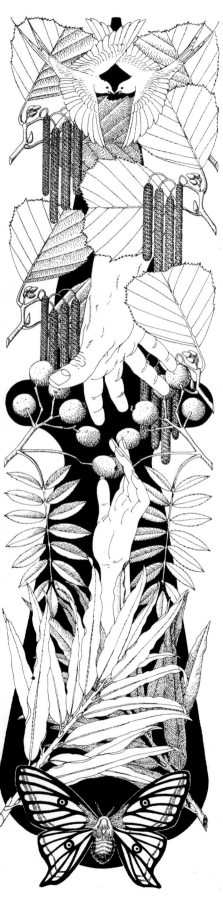

Orpheus and Eurydice

If Apollo was the greatest musician of the gods, Orpheus was supreme among the mortals. It was music from Orpheus's lyre which lulled the dragon that guarded the golden fleece to sleep and saved all but one of the Argonauts from the temptation of the Sirens. As a result, his fame had spread far and wide over the land of Thrace, where his father was king.

Orpheus was also a poet, whose inspiration came from the nine Muses, and a singer. At court, the people would listen spellbound as he sang the great sagas of his country, plucking the strings of his instrument in soft accompaniment. At times he would wander out into the countryside, playing as he went. The birds and wild beasts that roamed there would draw close to listen and to follow him. Even the trees swayed in time to the tunes he played.

It was while he was strolling alone through the woods that he met the beautiful dryad Eurydice and brought her back to the palace, to be his wife.

The dryads were nymphs of the trees and woods. Sometimes, when she was tired of her busy life at court, Eurydice would visit her former companions. They would sit on a grassy bank while she told them about her strange new city life, where there were hard, paved streets instead of the soft turf of the forest, and stone houses and temples instead of groves of trees. If Orpheus was with her the nymphs would dance and sing as he played to them.

At other times, Eurydice used to walk by herself through the woods, enjoying the dappled light which came down through the leaves above her and listening to the songs of the birds. She would stoop to pick the pink and mauve cyclamen and wood sorrel which grew beneath the trees and make garlands of their blossoms for her hair. Sometimes she would rest on the bank of a stream and watch butterflies dancing over the water. In the winter months she loved the rustle of the fallen leaves under her feet and would pause to run her hand over the rough bark of her beloved trees.

At times it snowed in that part of Greece. When this happened, Eurydice could see clearly the tracks of rabbits, hares, deer and of the larger beasts which preyed on them. Everything about her would be white. The familiar woods looked strange yet somehow even more beautiful. All around was silent; even the birds would stop singing. If, in the silence, a small gust of wind sent snow slithering down from the bare branches, Eurydice would start nervously.

One bright, warm summer's day when the sun was shining, she was watching a deer feeding in a grassy clearing when suddenly its ears pricked up and it raised its head. For a moment it stood like this, and then like a shadow it slipped away. A tall man whom Eurydice had never seen before strode from the trees into the clearing. He was handsome, but there was a cruel glint in his eyes which she did not like. He carried a bow and arrows across his back and stopped when he saw the girl standing there.

'I have heard of the nymphs of the Thracian woods, but you are the first I have seen,' he said. 'Everything that people say of their beauty is true if you are one of them.'

Eurydice was not vain and did not like to hear such flattery from a stranger. 'I thank you sir,' she said, 'but I suggest that you go on your way, for I have no wish to be disturbed.'

'You may be beautiful, but by the gods you have a sharp tongue!' the man answered. 'If you want to be rid of me, tell me first in which direction the deer I was stalking has gone. You must have seen it, for it came through here.'

Eurydice shook her head. 'No, sir,' she said. 'That I cannot tell you. It was too pretty to die.'

The man frowned. 'A nymph you may be but, by thunder, even the fairest nymphs do not defy a god! Tell me, I say!'

Stubbornly Eurydice shook her head. 'A god you may be,' she said, 'though I somehow doubt it, for if you were you would not behave so rudely. Take care how you speak to me, for my husband is the king's son and will not take kindly to someone who does not respect his wife.'

The stranger threw back his head and laughed. 'The wife of Orpheus, the poet and singer!' he exclaimed. 'I have heard he loves music more than battle. You threaten me with *him*? Clearly you do not know who I am.'

'No, sir,' Eurydice said, more calmly than she felt. 'I do not, and I do not wish to.'

'Nevertheless I will tell you,' said the stranger. 'Perhaps it will humble your proud spirit a little. I am Aristaeus, the god of hunters.'

'Then you should be more gentle,' answered Eurydice, 'for was not your own mother the nymph Cyrene? I have heard the story of how she was carried off from her home by Apollo and bore his son.'

'Gentle? Yes, my mother was gentle. But I learned from my father, the great Apollo, to take what I want when I want it.' The stranger paused and then added, gesturing to her: 'Come here! I will have a kiss from Orpheus's wife! Then we will see if he dares defy me!' He strode forward, and Eurydice, terrified, turned and fled.

Swiftly she ran through the trees, dodging first right then left. The low boughs brushed her face as she ran and, where the trees grew less thickly, brambles tore at her tunic as if to hold her back. But his life as a hunter had made Aristaeus a fine athlete and he ran as fast as she, crashing through thickets like a wounded boar. Eurydice could hear him behind her. Once she stumbled and thought that she would fall, but she regained her balance and ran on. Her voice echoed through the woods as she cried out desperately for help, but there was no one near to hear. The only answer was a cruel laugh from behind her.

The chase continued through mossy clearings and over half-hidden streams of clear water where the fish swam unconcerned in the shadows under the banks. Eurydice's heart was pounding, but it seemed at last that she was drawing away from her pursuer. As the ground began to rise and the trees became fewer, Aristaeus's footsteps grew more faint.

Presently, she scrambled upwards into the sunlight over a rock-strewn slope. At last the footsteps had ceased. Eurydice could not be sure that she had escaped and she continued upwards until, at the summit of the higher ground, she threw herself down exhausted on a flat-topped rock. Below her and all around she could see the green tops of the trees. From here she would be able to see Aristaeus a long way away, so she decided to rest for a while.

Eurydice saw no more of Aristaeus, and after a while she dozed in the hot sun. The whole world seemed to be at peace and drowsing. Suddenly another sun-lover appeared – a deadly viper which lived on the stony ground surrounding the place where the girl lay. It moved slowly over the warm earth by the flat-topped rock, its forked tongue darting in and out. As it passed near her, Eurydice stirred and turned in her sleep. One of her slender legs now barred the viper's path. The snake hissed and coiled its body quickly, raising its head to strike. Its fangs sank deep, spreading their venom, but Eurydice did not wake. A bee droned lazily by and was gone, and then no more sound was heard. The poison had done its deadly work.

Night came, and still Eurydice had not returned to the palace. At first Orpheus was not seriously worried, for no harm had ever come to his wife on her lonely wanderings in the woods where she was so much at home. But when midnight came, search parties were sent out to scour the surrounding countryside. Their calls echoed through the trees as they searched. Lights flickered here and there through the woods like phantoms. It was morning when they at last found her. Placing her body on a stretcher hastily made from saplings bound with creepers, the searchers carried her back to the palace with heavy hearts.

Orpheus was inconsolable. His father tried to comfort him but it was no use. Orpheus sat alone, playing sad tunes on his lyre and thinking only of his lost love.

But Aristaeus had been wrong about Orpheus. He was a brave man, braver by far than most, and perhaps his desperation to win back Eurydice gave him a greater courage than he would normally have had. For he decided that he would enter Hades itself and fetch her back to earth from there. Everyone tried to dissuade him. 'Not even in your wildest dreams should you consider going there' King Oeagrus told his son. 'The dead are the dead and the living the living. You are mad to think you can change the way of the gods. Those who go to the Underworld can never return.'

Nevertheless, Orpheus set out, his lyre slung from his shoulder, his mind full only of Eurydice. He journeyed overland to Aornum in Thesprotis, which borders the Ionian Sea. He had heard that a narrow passageway led from here, far beneath the earth, to the river Styx. The river was the

only barrier to Hades itself. He found the passage and descended out of the sunlight into the gloom. Water dripped from the dank ceiling and rats scuttled away into the dark corners as he made his way bravely forward. At last the Styx was before him. Charon the ferryman sat there in his boat, waiting for his next cargo of the dead.

Orpheus knew it would not be easy to persuade Charon to take a living cargo but, trusting to the magical powers of his music, he struck a note on his lyre. A rare smile lit the stern face of the boatman. He leaned back in his seat and his eyes closed as the music enveloped him, its wonderful harmonies echoing back from the cavernous walls. Few could have resisted its appeal for long, and Charon succumbed to it completely.

'I can deny nothing to one who can play as you can,' he said to Orpheus. 'I will take you over the river, though I may pay for it later when my master finds out what I have done.' Charon moved to one side to let Orpheus clamber into the boat.

On the other bank stood the guard dog Cerberus, but Orpheus's playing soothed even this fierce animal and Cerberus, like Charon, allowed him to pass.

In due course, Orpheus was brought before Persephone, the queen of the Underworld. Before he spoke he once more played his lyre, and the shades of the dead clustered near to hear his music. Persephone's heart was touched by his story and his music and she agreed to let Eurydice return to earth.

'But on one condition only,' she told Orpheus. 'She must follow behind you as you go. If you turn round to see her before she reaches the upper air, she must return here for ever.'

So Eurydice was brought to them and the young couple embraced while Persephone looked on with a half-smile, as if she already doubted her decision. But she did not change her mind. The pair crossed the Styx safely and began the long climb up the passage to the surface of the earth. Orpheus never looked back, though he was greatly tempted to make sure that the footsteps he could hear behind him really were those of his beloved wife and not some trickery of the shades. Up and up they climbed, until presently daylight showed ahead of them.

A few minutes later, Orpheus was at the mouth of the cave, and the warmth of the sun was on his face. A great joy flooded through his whole being. What had been only a wild dream of happiness regained had actually come true. He turned to take Eurydice in his arms. However, less strong than he, she had lagged some way behind him in the climb. He saw her dimly coming towards him, still in the shadowy passage. But even as he looked she seemed to fade away and then was gone. He rushed forward but it was too late. She had returned to the shadowy world of the dead and was lost to him forever.

The story of Arion, another famous musician, has a happier ending. Arion was a son of Poseidon, but lived in Corinth at the court of King Periander. Like Orpheus he was a renowned lyre player and he travelled far and wide to play and sing at the feasts and festivals of Greece.

Most of these festivals were held on the mainland, at the largest and most important towns, such as Tiryns, Mycenae, Athens and Thebes, and these did not involve Arion in more than a few days journey. However, there came a time when Arion received an invitation to compete in a festival in Sicily. It was to be an occasion of great importance, with the finest players from many lands gathering to take part. Arion decided that, though it meant a long sea voyage to reach the island, he could not miss it.

At the end of the festival, Arion was chosen as the victor. Long speeches were made in praise of his playing, and gifts were showered upon him – jewels, richly embroidered cloaks, gold ornaments, armlets and medallions of silver, and vases, bowls and drinking vessels painted and decorated by the finest artists of the day with colourful scenes from the lives of the gods.

Dressed in his new finery, Arion took his prizes packed in huge, metal-bound chests, and boarded the ship for the return journey. The ship sailed westward for two days. On the third morning, while Arion was strolling on the deck, he was suddenly seized by the sailors and dragged, struggling, before the captain. The captain, a bearded ruffian, smiled cruelly as he tore a silver medallion from about Arion's neck.
'I think that we can find a better use for all your treasures than to carry them back to Greece for you to enjoy,' he said, taking a dagger from the sash about his waist. Chuckling, he drew his thumb along the razor-sharp edge of the blade.

Arion saw that, surrounded by so many armed and ruthless men he stood no chance of resisting. But he stood up straight to show that he did not really fear death.
'If I am to die,' he said, 'let it be in my own way.'

The captain shrugged. It did not really matter to him how this rich stranger met his end, so Arion was allowed to mount the prow of the ship, where he played a few last defiant notes on his lyre before plunging into the waves.

So anxious were the captain and the sailors to get at the iron-bound chests and to gloat over the treasure inside them that they spared Arion no second glance. Had they done so, they would have seen a school of dolphins leaping through the waves near the ship. One of these took Arion on his back and sped away with him over the water. Soon they were far ahead of the ship, making for Greece.

Some days later the ship sailed into the harbour of Corinth and the captain related with great conviction how the passenger from Sicily had been swept overboard in a gale with all he possessed. The captain had just finished his story when he looked across the quay and his face went white. For there, walking slowly towards him, was the man who should now have been lying on the shifting sands far beneath the waves.

Arion said nothing to him, but walked purposefully past and up the gangway to the ship. The captain and crew were seized and led away in chains and Arion's treasure was carried safely away to the palace. It is said that in gratitude for his safe return, Arion ordered a fine bronze sculpture of a man riding a dolphin's back to be placed on the shore, just in the place where the real dolphins had left him.

Eros and Psyche

Eros, the son of Aphrodite, was the Greek god of love. In many of the myths, he is a charming child, but at the time this story took place, he had grown into a beautiful young man. Armed with a bow and a quiver full of arrows, he had the power to bring love to both gods and mortals. Anyone whose skin was even grazed by his arrow fell immediately in love with the very next person they saw.

'Tell me, Eros,' Aphrodite said to him one day 'do I grow old? Is my skin wrinkled? Does my hair show streaks of grey? Is my back bowed like that of an old crone?'

Eros was startled. This was not the sort of question he expected from someone who was the most beautiful woman in the world and who knew very well that she was. He did not know what was in his mother's mind, but he answered truthfully enough.

'No one is fairer than you, or ever will be. Did not Paris put even Hera and Athene in second place? But why do you ask?'

Aphrodite gave a satisfied smile and nodded. 'I did not really doubt your answer,' she said, 'but it seems the mortal, Psyche, does not agree. I have heard on good authority that she claims greater beauty. She boasts that of the two of us, she is the full moon and I am but a distant star whose feeble light pales before the radiance of her moonbeams.'

'She has a poetical turn of mind, at any rate,' remarked Eros. Aphrodite brushed this aside impatiently.

'She must be taught a lesson,' she said. 'Go to her and draw your bow. Aim well so that the arrow pierces her heart. And make sure that some hideous thing is standing by when she opens her eyes. I want her to suffer love for the most abominable creature in the world.'

Eros was not anxious to carry out the mission. He tried to argue but Aphrodite would not be swayed and at length he had to agree. However, as he crept up to Psyche sleeping among the flowers in a sunny meadow, he was so dazzled by her beauty that he stumbled on a stone and half fell beside her. The tip of one of his arrows sank deep into his own leg, and before he knew what was happening, he was hopelessly in love with her.

Eros knew he would have to be careful. Aphrodite must know nothing of his love and, since even the best of women gossip, it would be better if Psyche herself did not know who had won her. So he carried her, still sleeping, to his home. There he laid the girl gently down on a bed in one of the great sleeping chambers and left her to sleep. That night when darkness came, he visited her, but he did not light a lamp. Out of the gloom he said to her: 'Our love shall be greater than any which has ever been. Come to me and we will find happiness beyond imagining.'

'But who are you that speaks to me like this?' Psyche asked. It was not an unreasonable question, but her voice suggested that she was intrigued rather than alarmed.

'You must not ask that,' Eros told her. 'When the owls wing their silent way through the dark skies each night I will be with you, but you must never look at my face or try to discover my name. You must have trust.'

And so each night Eros and Psyche loved one another, and each morning, before the sun rose in the east, Eros was gone.

Time went by and Psyche's sisters came to visit her. They were scandalized by what she told them of her new life, but possibly a little jealous too. 'But surely, surely, you must have peeped? Just one small peep?' one of them asked. Psyche shook her head.

'If it was me I couldn't *bear* not to know who he is,' said another.

'Why, he might be the most fearsome monster, with seven heads,' said the first sister.

'And horns like a goat!'

'And snakes for hair!'

'With five wives already!'

'And fifty children, ten from each!'

The words tumbled out as one sister after another added horror on horror from the depths of their imaginations. But Psyche merely smiled.

However, when night came she could not rid her mind of her sisters' words. She felt in her heart that they could not be true, but even if they were not, she had many times wished to look on the marvellous being who came to her out of the darkness. So far she had been faithful to his trust, but one look – just one small glance – what harm could it do? So she reasoned to herself.

Before dawn next morning she awoke, with Eros sleeping beside her. She slipped from the bed and tiptoed from the room. Downstairs she lit a lamp and came softly back again, holding the lamp above the bed so that its soft light shone on the sleeping figure.

What she saw filled her with even greater happiness than before, for the young man was more beautiful than anyone she had ever seen. How she would tease her sisters about their doubts and suspicions!

Perhaps because the light disturbed him, Eros stirred and put his arm across his face. Psyche feared that he would wake. She did not want him to know that she had disobeyed him and in her haste to blow out the lamp, she spilled a drop of the hot oil on his arm. At once his eyes opened and he saw her standing over him.

As he looked his brow darkened, but he did not speak. She drew back, terrified by the angry scene she thought would follow. But Eros rose and, still in silence, left the room without another glance at her. She heard his footsteps on the stairs grow fainter. Then there was silence and she wept.

Later that morning her sisters saw Psyche's red-rimmed eyes and questioned her, but she would say nothing. Finally, she locked herself in her room to escape from them. Darkness came and she lay alone, listening to the noises of the night. Each sound, however slight, quickened the beating of her heart, but each one died away, until at last she knew her lover would not come again.

Over the many long, weary months that followed, Psyche roamed the world, looking for her lost love. At last, in desperation, she appealed to Aphrodite to help her.

'Goddess of love,' she prayed, 'You above all must understand what I am suffering. I have lost the one thing I valued, and just for curiosity's sake. Help me, please. Surely I have been punished enough for my foolishness.'

The gods did not easily forgive anyone they thought had wronged them, and Aphrodite was no exception.

'The man you love is my son, Eros,' she replied sternly. 'Why should a god love a foolish girl? However, it is just possible that he will return to you, but only if you first do exactly what I tell you.'

Psyche agreed gladly, but she did not know that the goddess had chosen tasks which she was certain the girl would not be able to perform.

First, Aphrodite took Psyche to a granary. On the floor was a large pile of grain, taller by far than either of them. The pile was a mixture of corn, rye and barley.

'See,' said Aphrodite, pointing. 'This grain is useless as it is. Sort one kind from another and make three separate piles. When it is done, come back to me.' Then she left and Psyche sat on the floor to begin the first of her tasks.

She started hopefully, but very soon began to feel that even if she lived for a thousand years she would never be able to finish. Nevertheless, picking one grain here, another there, she worked steadily for many hours. The three piles she was making never seemed to get much bigger and, after almost a whole day, each contained not much more than she could have held in one hand. She was just wondering whether to admit defeat when something caught her eye.

Across the floor, lit by a shaft of evening sunlight from the window, a column of ants was moving. She watched them as they approached the grain. Just before they reached it, the column split into three. Each ant in the first column took a grain of corn in its tiny pincer jaws and each of the second column took a grain of rye. The third column took barley and in a steady procession they scurried to and fro between the big pile of grain and the three smaller ones that Psyche had started to make. The small ones grew in size and the big pile diminished. When night came, the ants had finished. As silently as they had come, they formed a single column once more and marched away, leaving the sorted grains.

Aphrodite was bitterly angry when she found that the seemingly impossible task she had set had been completed so quickly. Of course she knew nothing about the ants, and Psyche did not tell her of their help. In fact Psyche found it hard to believe what had happened herself. She wondered if it could possibly have been Eros, taking pity on her, who had sent the ants to her. But no sign came to her that this was so, and she resigned herself to the next task, hoping it would help to win him back at last.

The second task was no less daunting than the first, for Aphrodite ordered Psyche to descend to the Underworld to fetch a casket of love. It was only after the goddess had left her that Psyche realized she had no idea how to get to the Underworld. In fact, if she had not chanced to meet Orpheus soon after he had returned from his own tragic journey, she might never have been able to begin her mission. As it was, he told her where the entrance to the passage he had used was and Psyche set off at once.

As she came with a message from the goddess Aphrodite, Charon the ferryman and Cerberus the guard dog allowed her to pass without question and she was summoned to appear before the Queen of the Underworld.

'Very well,' Persephone said when Psyche told her why she had come. 'Aphrodite may have the casket, but what it contains is for her eyes only. It must not be opened by anyone else.' And she handed the casket of love to the girl.

As Psyche made her way back up the gloomy passage she could not stop thinking about what Persephone had said. The temptation to look in the casket grew. She forgot completely how curiosity had ruined her life with Eros and thought only of the power the casket might give her: it might even, she thought, regain Eros's love for her. As soon as she emerged into the daylight, she lifted the casket's lid. But instead of beauty, the box contained eternal sleep. Psyche's eyes immediately grew heavy. She lay down on the grass, her eyes closed, and she slept.

Some say that after a long time Zeus took pity on her and brought her up to heaven, to be reunited once more with Eros. Perhaps this is true, or perhaps she still sleeps in the sunlight among the flowers, looking just as she did when her lover first found her. Who knows?

Pygmalion's statue

Aphrodite, the goddess of love and beauty, was worshipped by all the people of Cyprus, for she had made the island kingdom her own. The young king of Cyprus, Pygmalion, himself conducted the ceremonies of worship in her temple, but as well as being both priest and king he was a fine sculptor. In fact it was said that his work exceeded in skill even that of Daedalus the maze-maker, and that it was difficult to believe that the statues he made were not living beings.

Pygmalion had for a long time looked in vain for a bride whose beauty would match his idea of a perfect woman. It was a discouraging search, for all around him Pygmalion saw disastrous marriages. Many of his subjects had married the daughters of Propoetus, who deserted their husbands for any stranger who came their way. The men they had married were known as the Cerastea. Their wives were not only unfaithful to them, but also led them into evil ways. For instance, instead of sacrificing the traditional ox or bullock to Aphrodite, as they had done in the past, the Cerastea now invited people to their homes, killed them and offered them up to the goddess instead.

Not only Pygmalion but Aphrodite herself was disgusted by such acts. Her punishments were carefully selected: she turned the Cerastean men into bullocks which, in due course, would be sacrificed themselves. The hard and ruthless women she turned into stones, to match their stony hearts.

With examples like these before him, it was not surprising that Pygmalion hesitated in choosing a bride. In fact he did more than hesitate; he decided that he would never marry, but devote his time and the love he felt inside him to working on the most beautiful statues he could fashion. These he would present to Aphrodite to atone for the past wickedness of his people.

Such was the strength of his feeling and inspiration that his hand was guided as if by magic to create a wonderful marble statue. The statue was of a girl so perfect and so lovely that Pygmalion fell hopelessly in love with her. Day by day his love grew, and he adorned the statue with fine jewellery and garlands of flowers. But it remained a cold, marble figure beneath his touch.

At length the day of the feast of Aphrodite drew near. All Cyprus was on holiday and the people thronged from every part of the island to bring their offerings to the temple. With them, Pygmalion knelt before the goddess he had served so well and prayed that she would grant him the wish that was dearest of all to his heart: that his statue should be given life.

Though he received no sign, he returned home strangely elated, yet half fearful of what he would find. In his workshop the beautiful statue seemed as lifeless as before. It stood there still and cold, staring past him with its sightless eyes. In his despair Pygmalion embraced it, kissing the cold lips passionately. Then, exhausted and disillusioned, he lay down at its feet and fell asleep.

Towards morning, Pygmalion began to dream. Once again he returned from the ceremony, again he stood in front of his statue, and again kissed its cold lips. But this time everything was changed. As he touched the statue he felt the warmth of life flowing through the white, ivory-coloured body. She moved gently and he looked into lively blue eyes, returning his love. Soft arms enfolded him and as they did so, he opened his sleeping eyes.

All around him, the jumble of stones and tools, half-finished statues and carvings lay as before. But something was different. Where a cold marble woman had stood was a beautiful girl, bending lovingly towards him just as she had done in his dream. Before he could rub his eyes, Aphrodite herself appeared.

'You above all men deserve happiness,' she told the wondering king, 'a happiness you yourself have fashioned. Here before you is the queen you have sought so long. Love her well and guard her from harm.'

Echo and Narcissus

The nymph Echo sat alone on a hillside not far from Athens. She threw back her head and closed her eyes, feeling the caress of a soft breeze on her cheek and letting the warm spring sunshine play on her face. Her golden hair hung behind her, moving softly in the gentle air.

After a while she sat forward, clasping her arms around her knees and looking towards the trees of a small wood below her. On the rocky slope which led down to it lived a flock of hoopoes, their short, curved beaks probing for ants in the dry, sandy soil between the rocks. Their pale chestnut colouring contrasted vividly with the green of the trees beyond, and the black tips to the feathers of their crests glistened as they raised and lowered their heads.

As Echo rose to her feet, they took wing and moved in a flock across the hillside, settling again some distance away. Echo watched them for a moment and then wandered slowly down into the shade of the trees. Soon she heard voices not far away. A man and a girl were talking, and the nymph decided to see who they were without letting them know she was there. She suspected that their meeting might be a romantic one and, with thoughts of love never far from her own mind, she could not resist seeing if the girl was one of her fellow nymphs.

She moved quietly through the trees. Soon she was peering from behind some bushes down into a small hollow. As she had suspected, there, sitting on a mossy bank was a nymph she knew. But when Echo saw whose arm was around her, she gasped in alarm, for she recognized him as the great god Zeus. Slowly she backed away, fearful of what Zeus might do if he found out that she was spying on him. When she was at a safe distance she once more strolled on, feeling greatly relieved.

There was seldom anyone except nymphs in the wood, but presently Echo saw a tall, handsome woman in a purple cloak coming her way, and her heart once more beat with fear, for she knew who this was, too. It was Hera, Queen of Heaven, Zeus's wife. The expression on Hera's face showed that she was far from pleased.

'Tell me, nymph,' she said. 'Have you seen my husband pass this way, perhaps not alone. I believe he is somewhere nearby and I need to find him quickly.'

'How would I know him, please, if I did see him?' Echo asked. Of course she knew the answer, but was terrified of being involved in a dispute between Zeus and Hera. Their passionate quarrels were well known. Wise people kept well away at such times.

Hera looked closely at the girl, rightly suspecting that she was not as innocent as she seemed. 'Why, my husband is Zeus,' the goddess said. 'Come! Don't tell me that you, a nymph, would not know *him*.'

'I think that I would know him, now that I know who *you* are,' said Echo, 'but I have been wandering in this wood all morning and there is no one here but me.'

Hera was at last convinced. She turned and went away in the direction from which she had come. Once back on Olympus, however, she looked down and saw Zeus and the nymph, arms entwined, walking from the wood.

The goddess's beautiful face was contorted with rage. Echo had deceived her, that was clear, and she must suffer for it. So Hera put upon her a terrible curse that prevented her from speaking and singing as she had loved to do. All she could do from that moment was to repeat the last few words of what others said to her.

Living in the same part of the country at that time was the youth Narcissus, the son of a river god and a nymph. He was a fine-looking young man, so handsome that every girl who saw him fell desperately in love with him. But his mother had spoiled him. She had told him so often that he was far too good-looking to waste his time with the local girls that he believed her. In fact, in his mind he went further than this, and his vanity grew day by day until he decided that no woman on earth could possibly be worthy of him.

Soon his friends could put up with his conceit no longer and one by one they abandoned him. Narcissus, however, was quite content with his own company. One day he was wandering in the woods where Echo had met Hera. Echo was there again, a sad, lonely figure, who now kept to herself since she could not speak with her friends. She saw Narcissus standing in a shaft of sunlight which shone down through the trees and knew at once that he was the love of her life.

She came up to him, longing to speak, but he motioned her away. He had been imagining that he was one of the gods of Olympus, and did not want his dream to be disturbed.

'Leave me alone, girl,' he said contemptuously. 'Can't you see that you are disturbing me?'

'. . . are disturbing me,' Echo answered.

'I am disturbing *you*? What nonsense you talk.'

'. . . nonsense you talk,' Echo answered.

'There is no call for insolence.' Narcissus told her. 'If you knew who I am you would be more polite.

It's time you nymphs became more respectful.'

'. . . more respectful,' Echo answered.

'That is better,' said Narcissus. ' But all you girls are the same. All you want is to make love to me.'

'. . . make love to me,' Echo answered.

' Just as I thought. You are like all the rest. I wish you farewell,' and, so saying, Narcissus turned and strode away.

'. . . farewell,' Echo answered helplessly.

Narcissus went on through the wood and presently he came to a clearing where a fountain played. Nearby were ornamental pools where the water was as still and clear and smooth as the finest mirror. Narcissus was thirsty so he knelt down by one of the pools to drink. He cupped his hands and bent forward, but then paused, staring in amazement into the water. For looking up at him was the most beautiful face he had ever seen. He had no idea that it was his own reflection. His heart beat fast, and he knew that he had been right to wait for someone worthy of himself before he fell in love.

For a long time he crouched there, simply staring at his reflection, growing more enchanted with it every minute. Then he spoke and was puzzled when no reply came, though the stranger's lips had moved. Surely it could not be that the person before him did not feel as he did? He spoke again, but still there was no answer. He bent still further down to kiss the lips which moved but from which no sound came, and at once the beautiful face was shattered.

Narcissus remained motionless. After a while the pool resumed its calm and the face came again. He bent once more to kiss it, but the same thing happened again. Yet again he tried, and gave a cry of temper when the face vanished for the third time.

'You have rejected me!' he cried. 'I cannot live without you!' So saying, he drew his dagger and plunged its sharp point into his breast. 'Farewell, beloved one,' he called as he fell, and far away among the trees an echo came:

'. . . beloved one!'

Narcissus lay dead, but though he had been vain and selfish, he *had* been a beautiful man, and the gods were sad to see him disappear for ever. In the place were his blood sank into the ground a new flower appeared, with white petals and a clear red centre. The flower head on its long stalk danced in the light wind, which rippled its reflection in the pool water, and to this day the flower bears Narcissus's name.

Midas, the golden king

Midas, King of Phrygia, was a foolish, greedy man. One day Silenus, leader of the satyr band which roamed the world with Dionysus, came to the door of the royal palace. He was tired and hungry, for he had lost his way and had been wandering in the hills for some days. Midas made him welcome and gave the satyr food and shelter. Silenus stayed with him a week and on his last night the king ordered a magnificent banquet. Together with the noblemen of the court, they feasted long into the night, and in the morning Silenus prepared for his departure.

'You have been more than generous in your hospitality,' he told Midas, 'and I thank you. Tell me, is there anything you have been wanting for a long time? I would very much like to give you something as a token of my thanks.'

Midas's greedy eyes gleamed. A new chariot, emblazoned with jewels? One hundred fine stallions from the plains of Lydia? Five hundred head of cattle from Arcadia? All these and many other things went swiftly through his mind, but he was afraid to voice his thoughts aloud. Silenus might be thinking of something even more magnificent, which he would not get if he named a lesser gift. On the other hand, supposing it were only something like a decorated bronze drinking vessel that Silenus had in mind? Midas did not know what to do, but he knew that he must speak soon or the satyr would be offended. Then he might get nothing.

'I – I do not know,' he said at length. 'Let the choice be yours.'

Silenus nodded. 'Very well,' he said. 'You may make one wish and whatever it is shall be granted. Think well before you make it, for there are many things in this world to choose from.'

So saying, Silenus went on his way, but even before he had finished speaking Midas had made up his mind. He would wish that everything he touched should be turned to gold. He would be rich beyond all imagining, a king among kings, and all men would come to pay tribute to his greatness. He made his wish and was delighted by what happened. He touched a chair and it turned instantly to solid gold. Then he touched a table and the drinking vessels on it, and his robe, which he had to remove quickly for its weight in gold bore him down. He laughed with pleasure and rushed out, running from room to room in the palace, touching everything he saw. All turned to gold. Soon the palace gleamed as if a hundred suns shone from the high ceilings.

At length Midas grew tired, for he was not used to such exertions. The

time for his midday meal was approaching and he sat down on a golden chair at the golden table in the room where he had said farewell to Silenus. A servant brought him fruit and set it before him, and as Midas touched the platter on which it lay, it became gold. He laughed happily. Then he lifted a bunch of grapes to his mouth. As he did so his expression suddenly changed to one of dismay, for the grapes were grapes no longer: they were small, golden balls, gleaming and appetizing but quite impossible to eat. He threw them from him and ordered meat to be brought, but again the same thing happened. Angrily, he pushed away the servant who stood waiting beside him. At once, a golden statue with staring, sightless eyes, replaced the servant's warm, living body.

Midas rushed from the room and down through the palace kitchens to the storerooms where the food was kept. He touched a sack of grain and instantly it was gold. He moved along the shelves of storage jars, touching each one, and they became golden too. In his despair, he threw himself on the floor and wept as the true meaning of the satyr's gift became clear to him.

Days went by and his despair and hunger grew. He could not sleep or eat. When he embraced his children they turned instantly to golden figures. Even the tears that fell from his eyes dropped heavily to the golden floor. At length he consulted an oracle and its words gave him hope.

'Go at once to the banks of the river Pactolus,' the oracle told him, 'and bathe in its waters. The curse of the gold will be lifted from you. It is hoped that you have learned your lesson.'

Midas did as the oracle had suggested. The curse was lifted and the sands of the river bed from that time onwards gleamed with the gold which he had shed. He went back to the palace, determined to behave very differently in future.

King Midas, however, did not gain much sense from his experience – although he did lose his love of gold. No one but a very foolish mortal would have agreed to act as judge in a contest between two of the gods, for their jealousy of successful rivals was well known. Yet this is just what Midas did.

Apollo had already been acclaimed the greatest of all musicians in a competition with Marsyas the satyr. Pan would not accept this, and he issued a challenge. Each god would play in turn, and Midas would decide the winner.

Apollo first played his lyre, the clear notes singing out through the woods until even the noisy birds were silent, acknowledging his supremacy. Then Pan raised his mournful pipes, making a sad, mysterious and discordant sound that sent the squirrels scurrying into the trees. Midas knew by now that whichever god lost the contest would punish the judge, not the victor. However, to his ears, Pan's music was best and it was to Pan that he turned with the laurel crown.

Apollo stamped his foot in rage. 'Stupid and toneless mortal,' he roared. 'A man with your judgement should have ears to match. Take these. Ass's ears are just what you need.'

Clapping his hands to his head in horror, Midas found long, pointed furry ears sprouting and growing from its sides. He covered them hastily with his cloak and stole secretly back to his palace.

Long, furry ears did not led dignity to a king and Midas knew that he would be a figure of fun. He tried wearing the largest hat he could find in his wardrobe, with the ears tied up inside it. On state occasions in the future, however, he would have to wear his crown. And in the meantime he could not very well keep the hat on in bed. In the morning when his servants came to wake him, they would see the ears and laugh behind his back. So Midas barred the servants from his room and concealed his ears as best he could until such time as his hair had grown long and thick. At least then his ears could not be seen. But he had come to look like a wild man from the mountains and the hair became so unmanageable that he had to send for the royal barber.

The barber snipped away and combed and parted and soon, of course, he saw the ears. He said nothing to the king, but found such a secret about his royal master hard to keep to himself.

At length the barber made up his mind and went out to the river bank where Midas had washed away his gold. The ground was sandy there, and he went down on his knees and scooped a hole in it. Into this he whispered his secret: 'King Midas has the ears of an ass.'

Then, greatly relieved, he pushed the sand back so that the words would be buried for ever. After a time, a clump of reeds grew on the spot, and from that time, whenever the wind blew gently through them, they whispered this question: 'Who is it that has the ears of an ass?'

Back would come the answer: 'Midas, the king!'

The death of the Chimaera

Bellerophon, a young prince from the city of Corinth, lived for some
while at the court of Proetus, at that time king of Argos. While he
was there, the king's young wife Anteia fell in love with him. As soon
as Bellerophon discovered her feelings for him, he decided to avoid
her whenever possible, but he did not leave the court altogether.
For a long time Anteia persisted in seeking him out, but at last she
became annoyed at his rejection and planned to take her revenge.
Putting on her most innocent expression, she told her husband that
Bellerophon had made advances to her – the exact reverse of the truth.

Proetus believed what his wife told him and was, of course,
extremely angry. However, the laws of hospitality did not allow him to
kill his guest. Instead, he hid his feelings and asked Bellerophon to
take a letter to Anteia's father, Iobates. The letter was sealed and
Bellerophon naturally had no idea what it contained. In fact it told
Iobates that Bellerophon was a dangerous adulterer and asked that he
should be put to death without delay; the honour of Iobates's
daughter was at stake.

For some reason, Iobates was reluctant to carry out the murder
himself, but he quickly thought of a plan which he hoped would have
the same result. Putting the letter he had just read in his belt, he
strolled across the room to the window, where Bellerophon was
standing.

'My son-in-law tells me that you are a brave man,' he said. 'You may
be the very one I have been looking for.'

Bellerophon looked at him questioningly.

'There is a monster not far from here,' went on Iobates, 'which has
been troubling us for some time. It is known as the Chimaera and is
half a lion, half a goat, with a viper for a tail. It was fathered, they say,
by the serpent-headed Typhon. I want it destroyed, but none of my
people dares face it. Now if you are the man that Proetus says you
are . . .'

Iobates left the sentence unfinished, but his meaning was clear
enough to Bellerophon. If he did not offer to fight the Chimaera, he
would be branded a coward. Without a moment's hesitation,
Bellerophon accepted the challenge. Iobates, however, had not been
entirely truthful. The Chimaera was far more terrifying than he had
described it. Its lion's head breathed fire like a dragon so that it was
impossible to attack from close by, while it had the agility of a
mountain goat in twisting and turning to avoid a well aimed arrow. Its

viper tail lashed out at any attacker, spitting poison from its deadly fangs. Many of Iobates's best soldiers had already tried and failed to conquer it.

Before he set out to find the Chimaera, Bellerophon took advice from a soothsayer. He was told that he could succeed only if he was mounted on the winged stallion Pegasus. Pegasus was the offspring of Poseidon and the gorgon Medusa. Although he had sprung from the monster's severed, snaky head, he was far from being monstrous himself. His fine, strong horse's body was more beautiful than any ordinary stallion, while the great wings that sprang from his shoulders carried him through the air more gracefully than a bird.

Before Bellerophon could ride him, Pegasus must first be caught and broken to the bit and bridle, for he lived wild and free.

That evening, as Bellerophon was journeying to Corinth, the goddess Athene appeared to him. In her hand she held a golden bridle.
'Take this,' she told Bellerophon, 'for without it you will never be able to tame so spirited a horse as Pegasus.'

Bellerophon managed to catch hold of Pegasus's mane while he was drinking at a spring. He slipped the golden bridle over his head, and held it firmly as the horse snorted and stamped at the unaccustomed restraint. Before long, however, he accepted Bellerophon on his back and together they flew up into the sky.

Pegasus's widespread wings carried them swiftly for many miles until Bellerophon saw below them on a high plateau the hideous shape of the Chimaera. He reined in Pegasus to steady him and then they swooped down, skimming low above the monster as it roared its defiance at them and tried to claw them out of the air. As they passed, Bellerophon shot arrow after arrow from his bow, until he could see that the monster was weakened. Bellerophon spurred Pegasus on for the final attack.

For this, he had prepared himself in an unusual way. Athene had warned him that the Chimaera breathed fire from its lion's mouth and he had prepared a special weapon. Cautiously he and Pegasus approached the monster and, as the great jaws with their deadly rows of teeth gaped wide to swallow them, Bellerophon thrust his spear deep between them. On the end of the spear he had fixed a large lump of lead. The flames which came roaring from the monster's throat could not reach Bellerophon, safe in the air on Pegasus's back, but they quickly melted the lead. It trickled in a searing stream into its stomach and the Chimaera died a hideous death.

When Bellerophon returned home victorious, Iobates began to doubt for the first time that such a man could have behaved in the dishonourable way his daughter had described. Nevertheless he set Bellerophon several more dangerous tasks and it was not until these has been successfully accomplished that he made up his mind that he had been wrong. Finally, he told Bellerophon all about Anteia's letter and when he heard the real explanation, offered the hand of his second daughter to make amends. With great celebrations, the two were married.

Bellerophon was now a grand and much respected citizen, universally admired for his bravery. People flattered him and exaggerated the stories of his exploits, and as time went by he began to think that everything they said was true. He grew unbearably conceited and when someone compared him to one of the gods he did not deny that he was worthy of the compliment. He came to believe that he really was the equal of the immortals. And if this was so, he reasoned, why should he not visit them on Olympus?

When Zeus heard this, he could hardly believe that a mere mortal would even think of coming uninvited to the heights of Olympus and he decided to teach Bellerophon a lesson.

Meanwhile down below Bellerophon had dressed himself in his finest robes and, mounting Pegasus he rode out of his stable yard to the top of a small hill. From there the winged horse sprang easily into the air. Up and up they went until the countryside below them was spread out like a gigantic map. Soon they were among the clouds and the smaller mountains were already far below. Still they climbed, up towards the distant peak of Olympus.

While Bellerophon was still some way off, Zeus released a tiny gadfly into the upper air. Straight as an arrow it flew to its target, and stung Pegasus viciously beneath his tail. The startled horse swerved and reared and with a terrible cry Bellerophon slipped from his back. He tried to clutch at the flying mane, but it slipped from his grasp. Down he fell to the earth far below.

Zeus chuckled heartlessly to himself as he watched Pegasus kicking his heels in his regained freedom: 'So perish all those who seek to rival the gods,' he said.

The fall of Troy

The tale of the siege of Troy is also the story of the final days of the great Greek heroes. Many did not survive its ten long years. The few who returned to Greece, weary from what had seemed an endless campaign, found that things had changed in their absence and that others, far less worthy than themselves, were ruling in their places. Gradually the noble families of the past declined and vanished.

The great war of Troy was caused when Paris, the young son of Troy's King Priam, kidnapped Helen, the wife of Menelaus, king of Sparta. Helen was the most beautiful woman in the world, and a daughter of Zeus. Some said that she ran away willingly with Paris, others that she was forced against her will. Whatever the truth of the matter, Paris refused to return her to her husband and she remained in Troy.

Many of the Greek kings and all her greatest warriors formed an alliance and sailed with their armies to humble Troy and to bring Helen back. So the Trojan war began.

The story of this massive campaign is, not surprisingly, a complicated one. Many separate incidents and battles went to make up the whole. Most of those who took part were soldiers whose names have long been forgotten. The wives and families of the leaders of each side were also heavily involved in the progress of the war, but their roles were in the main those of supporting players. Even the gods took sides, some supporting the Greeks, some the Trojans. But it is the great leaders themselves whose names have come down to us in the stories and literature of ancient Greece.

The commander of the Greek armies was the mighty Agamemnon, king of Mycenae, and brother to Helen's husband Menelaus. The greatest of the individual Greek warriors was Achilles. Among those who rallied their own armies for the sake of Helen and the honour of Greece were Diomedes, whose soldiers were the men of Argos and Tiryns, and Ajax, captain of the Locrians. Patroclus, the friend of Achilles, and the cunning Odysseus, who joined the war at a later stage, are also important in the story.

The Trojans were ruled by Priam, king of Troy, but as he was too old to fight himself, the defending forces came under the command of his eldest son, Hector. A younger branch of the family was represented by Aeneas, the only mortal in the legends of Greece whose mother was a goddess: he was the son of Aphrodite. During the course of the war, allies came to the help of Troy from other countries. The most

important of these were Penthesileia, queen of the Amazons, Sarpedon and Glaucus, leaders of the Lycians, and Rhesus from Thrace in the far north.

Another important Trojan was Cycnus. His father, Poseidon, had built the walls of Troy with Apollo, for an earlier king, Laomedon. Laomedon had refused to pay for the work after it was completed and had therefore angered the gods, but the building was of the very best and the fortifications were almost impregnable. Troy was situated on a low plateau in the country of Phrygia in Asia Minor, across the Aegean Sea from Greece. A wide plain spread out before it, and in the distance could be seen the narrow waters of the Hellespont.

As we have seen, Achilles was the greatest of the Greek fighters. His mother was the nereid Thetis. Long before, Poseidon had fallen in love with her but it was written that her son would be greater than his father, and he had married her sister instead. Now Zeus planned a marriage for Thetis and sent Hermes to earth to arrange it.

The chosen man was Peleus, a king's son who had been banished unjustly after the accidental death of his younger brother. He was now living with his old tutor, Chiron the centaur.

Hermes found Peleus sitting with Chiron outside the cave one evening.
'Greetings, Peleus,' he said, saluting them. 'And to you, good Chiron. I come from Zeus with news which will gladden your hearts, for Peleus has been chosen by the mightiest of the gods for a special honour.'

They made a place for Hermes by the fire in the mouth of the cave and he told them of Zeus's decree. Peleus was delighted, for he had heard how Thetis's beauty turned all men's heads and that many had tried unsuccessfully to win her. 'But how can I succeed where so many have failed?' he asked. 'Why should she favour me?'

Hermes laughed. 'Things that seem impossible may be done,' he said, 'if you know the secret. There is always an answer.' He told Peleus just what he must do.

So Peleus went down to the shore of the Myrtoan Sea, where Hermes had said that Thetis could be found. He hid himself, and when the nymph came from the water to walk on the sands, Peleus rushed out and seized her. At once she turned herself into a bird, but Peleus held it fast in his hands. The bird became a snake, but though it writhed and hissed it could not free itself from his grasp. Then the snake became a

dolphin, fighting for freedom in his arms. But no matter what form the nymph assumed in her efforts to escape, Peleus would not let go. At last Thetis gave up, became herself once more and consented to marry Peleus.

The wedding was held in Chiron's cave and many of the gods came to Mount Pelion to attend the celebrations. Among them were Hera, Athene and Aphrodite, and it was during these festivities that Paris chose Aphrodite as the most beautiful of all the goddesses. From that time, Aphrodite helped Paris whenever she could. Since her son Aeneas was also a Trojan, Troy had gained a powerful protectress.

In due time a son was born to Peleus and Thetis and they called him Achilles. They were immensely proud of the child and gave him everything he wanted. But Thetis, being a nereid, had ambitions for the baby that went beyond those of most mortal mothers. She wanted to make him immortal like herself and to make his body invulnerable, so that no human weapon could hurt him. First she took the child on the long journey under the earth to the Underworld, and there dipped him in the slowly-moving waters of the river Styx. Thetis dared not let go of her baby son completely, so she held him by one tiny heel, not realizing that this would remain dry. Though the river made the rest of his body safe from any weapon, his heel remained a danger point: a well aimed arrow with a poisoned tip could pierce its skin and bring death.

To bring Achilles immortality, Thetis carried out the ancient ritual of searing away his mortality by fire. She had not told Peleus of her intentions and was holding the baby in the flames when her horrified husband found her. Of course he flew into a rage and accused her bitterly of trying to kill the child. He would not listen when she tried to explain so, while he slept, she took the baby and ran away. She went straight to Mount Pelion and placed him in the care of Chiron the centaur, who had trained so many of the heroes of the past.

Achilles grew into a fine, handsome young man and Chiron could tell that of all those he had taught over the years, this son of Peleus and Thetis promised to be the noblest and most courageous warrior of all. Thetis visited the cave in the mountain from time to time, for she loved her son dearly.

When Thetis heard that Helen had been stolen away to Troy, she was deeply concerned. The great king Agamemnon had sent out a rallying call to all the fighting men of Greece. They were to join him at the port of Aulis on the Boeotian coast, where he was assembling a fleet of ships to sail against Troy. Thetis knew that if Achilles heard the summons he, like all Chiron's pupils, would answer it immediately. She hurried to Mount Pelion.

The news was there before her, and she found Achilles already preparing to depart. 'Enough warriors have already pledged themselves to overrun a hundred Troys' she told Achilles. 'There is no need for you to go as well.'

Her son could not agree. 'No victory is won until the battle has been fought,' he declared. 'No one can foretell the outcome with certainty. Agamemnon is a wise commander and if he says that men are still wanted, I must go.'

Chiron sided with the young man, and Thetis realized that she would not get her way by arguing. She therefore cast a spell over Achilles and took him away by stealth. She dressed him in the clothes of a girl and sailed with him to the island of Skyros. There she presented him to King Lycomedes as her daughter and left him in the king's care.

Meanwhile, the Greek kings and princes were gathering at Aulis. One after another, their armies marched into the city to salute Agamemnon before moving out into the surrounding countryside to make camp. Those from the nearby states arrived first. The troops from Arcadia and Messenia, even further to the south, and from Thessaly in the north, marched for many weeks to reach the gathering point. While the armies massed, the ships which were to carry them to Troy sailed in from the islands and from the coastal towns of the mainland. There was constant activity as they were prepared for war and loaded up with stores.

Odysseus of Ithaca was not among the early arrivals. He was reluctant to join the expedition at all, for he had married only the previous year and did not want to leave his wife and son. He had been warned by an oracle that many long years would pass before any of the warriors would return to Greece. So when Agamemnon travelled to Ithaca to persuade Odysseus to join him, Odysseus pretended he had gone mad. He yoked an ass and an ox to his plough and, with this strange, unbalanced team, tilled his fields, then sowed them with salt instead of grain.

Agamemnon suspected that Odysseus had a sane enough reason for acting as he did. He arranged for Odysseus's baby son Telemachus to be placed on the ground, right in the path of the plough. The father's reaction was anything but that of a madman. He reined in the ox and ass without a thought and rushed forward to pick the baby up, soothing its startled cries with very normal sounding words. After this it was difficult to pretend that his mind was deranged. Embracing his wife, he said farewell to his family and left with Agamemnon for Aulis.

At last everything was ready at Aulis. To a heralds' fanfare, the ranks of soldiers boarded the ships and the white sails were unfurled. Slowly the fleet moved out of the harbour and set off across the wide Aegean Sea towards Troy.

At first, the expedition seemed doomed to failure. The wind rose and great storms lashed the ships. They drifted helplessly before mountainous waves, far off their intended course. Many ships became separated from the main fleet and it was not until several days after the gales had died away that they all reassembled. The ships were in a sorry state, their sails torn or blown away, their masts broken, lying in a tangle of rigging on the deck. The oarsmen were exhausted and many of the stores were ruined with water. Clearly, the expedition could not proceed as it was, and there was nothing for it but to return to Greece to repair the ships.

There was another reason for going back, too. During the storm, Agamemnon had remembered that Calchas the seer had told him Troy would not fall unless Achilles was among the Greek warriors. When Achilles could not be found, Agamemnon had disregarded the prophecy, but now he could no longer ignore it.

As soon as the army was safely back at Aulis, Agamemnon set out to find the missing man. At last a rumour reached him that Achilles was on Skyros, living as a girl at Lycomedes's court. Odysseus, who was to be the principal maker of plans for the rest of the war, suggested a way of finding out if this were true.
'If he is there, he may be living willingly as a girl, or he may be held prisoner. It is possible that he knows nothing of our expedition. But until we are certain, we must be cautious.'

Odysseus bought gifts for Lycomedes and set out for Skyros with another Greek captain, Diomedes. They were in disguise, for it was part of their plan that no one should know who they were. If Achilles was being deliberately hidden, it would be better if they did not appear as warriors who had come to take him by force.

King Lycomedes welcomed the two travellers and did not seem in the least disturbed when they told him as much of the truth as they thought wise.

'When he heard we were coming to Skyros, King Agamemnon asked us to enquire if Achilles, son of Peleus, is living here. A great expedition to Troy is being prepared and it cannot succeed without Achilles. So the gods have spoken. Agamemnon's men have searched the mainland for him without success. Now we hear he may have left it altogether for one of the islands.'

Lycomedes shook his head at Odysseus's explanation. He had never found out that Thetis had deceived him.

'I am sorry, but I cannot help you,' he said. 'Achilles's sister is here, certainly, but she has had no news of him for a long while.'

Odysseus pretended to accept what the king told him. 'Our next call is at Seriphos,' he said. 'We will try our luck there. Meanwhile, here are some gifts for you and for your daughters from Agamemnon.'

The gifts were unwrapped – gold goblets for Lycomedes and necklaces, brooches, rings and fine embroidered cloths for the women of the household. The men placed them all in glittering piles on the long wooden table and the girls were summoned to make their choice. With delighted cries, Lycomedes's daughters clustered round, picking up one trinket after another. One girl held back. She was far taller than her companions and had a straight, slim figure; she seemed to have only a passing interest in all the finery. Then, as she fingered a crimson cloak which lay among the gifts, her mood seemed suddenly to change. Hidden carefully under the cloak was a richly jewelled sword. The girl seized it by the hilt with a practised hand and brandished it at the others in mock attack.

Odysseus knew that his plan had succeeded. 'Achilles,' he cried out, 'I am Odysseus, son of Laertes and my companion is Diomedes of Argos and Tiryns. We come from King Agamemnon to call you to the greatest battle of all time. Come to Troy with us and bring honour to yourself and to Greece.'

At that moment the spell which Thetis had cast over her son was broken. Achilles strode over to Odysseus and clasped his hand. 'I am with you,' he said firmly. 'Let the battle begin.' And he ran off to change from the women's clothes that now looked strange even to Lycomedes. Shortly afterwards the three men set off on their journey back to Aulis.

As soon as Achilles had rallied his soldiers to his banner and marched them swiftly from Thessaly, the Greek fleet set sail once more. This time the voyage was smooth. As the Greeks entered the straits of the Hellespont and drew close to the shore, they could see the Trojan army drawn up to prevent them from landing. But the Greeks drove onwards towards the beach. When they reached it, the crews leaped into the shallow water under a rain of arrows, hurtling spears and stones. Sword clashed on sword, and the din of battle increased as both sides threw themselves into the fight. Achilles was among the first ashore and, under his leadership the Greeks gradually forced the Trojans back from the sea's edge. Achilles seemed to be everywhere, scarcely noticing the danger, glad only to be a man among men once more. For a moment the Trojans seemed to hesitate, as if uncertain whether to fight or run. Then the tall figure of Cycnus, Poseidon's son, strode along their lines, urging them on to greater efforts, setting an example with his sword that few could equal.

Achilles knew that with a leader like this to inspire the other side, this first battle would be a costly one; and it was vital for the Greeks to gain at least a base for their camp on the shore. He hurled his spear at the tall Trojan. As the son of a god, however, Cycnus could not be killed by a mortal's spear, however dangerously it was aimed and however strong the arm that threw it. Though the spear struck him full on the chest, its point simply shattered and he was left unharmed. Achilles, with his own gift of invulnerability, guessed Cycnus's secret. He hacked his way through the Trojan ranks until the two men stood face to face. Those around drew back to watch the terrible duel.

Instead of thrusting with his sword or spear, Achilles held his sword by the blade and swung it round in a great arc, so that the hilt sent Cycnus's shield flying and struck him like a thunderbolt on the side of his head. Dazed, Cycnus staggered backwards and fell, and Achilles sprang on him like a panther. He wrenched at the Trojan's helmet and pulled the strap tight about his throat. Cycnus struggled, but Achilles's strength was like that of a god,

and he held on until Cycnus's body went limp. He did not die, however. A great white swan rose majestically from the ground where his body lay, flapping slowly out over the sea, and settling far out on the waves. Poseidon had reclaimed his son.

Perhaps the Trojans took this as a bad omen, or perhaps they were simply downcast and discouraged by the death of one of their bravest leaders. At any rate, they now withdrew to the shelter of the city walls. From there they watched the Greek armies setting up their camp, landing their stores, their horses and the chariots of war from the ships. The first battle of the war had been fought and victory had gone to Agamemnon. The Greek soldiers were in a buoyant mood, ready to finish the fight there and then. But one battle does not win a war, as their leaders knew only too well. This was only the opening chapter.

During the next few days there were only light skirmishes, as both sides buried their dead and took stock of the situation. In a last effort to avoid bloodshed, Menelaus sent an emissary to King Priam, challenging Paris to fight him to the death in single combat. If Menelaus won, Helen would be returned to him. If he lost, he would die an honourable death and Paris would have won Helen in a fair fight. Whatever happened, the Greek armies would then return home and Troy would be left in peace.

Paris accepted the challenge. He and Menelaus fought long and hard beside the gates of the city. At length a mighty blow from Menelaus's sword wounded Paris in the thigh and he fell to the ground. Before Menelaus could deliver his final blow, Trojan soldiers rushed from the gates, surrounded Paris and dragged him to safety. The great gates closed behind them and Menelaus stood there alone, baffled and angry at this behaviour.

The minutes passed, but the gates of Troy remained closed tight, and there was no sign of Helen. Obviously the Trojans had no intention of keeping their side of the bargain. He waited a while longer, then turned and walked furiously back to the Greek camp, refusing to speak to anyone as he passed through the ranks of the watching soldiers. However, he spoke long and bitterly on the subject of Greek honour at a council of war held later that night in Agamemnon's tent. All his companions agreed that the war must now run its course and that no more overtures of peace should be made in the future.

Their resolution was tested again and again during the years that followed, and there were many who argued that the Greeks should abandon a war they could never win. Though they held Troy in a state of seige, the walls Poseidon had built proved too strong for their attacks. From time to time the Trojans came out to fight on the plain, but as both sides were equally brave, no real gains were made.

Though Troy itself refused to yield, the Greeks spent much of the time raiding the neighbouring districts and towns which were loyal to the Trojan capital. As well as collecting food for their own army, the Greeks aimed to cut off all supplies of food and water from Troy itself. If the Trojan forces could be completely isolated and starved for long enough, they would soon be too weak to fight. Surrender could well come after, at most, a token struggle. The Greek soldiers tried hard to guard all the escape routes, but Trojan foraging parties still managed to slip through enemy lines by night, helped, of course, by their superior knowledge of the countryside.

One day Achilles was leading a cattle-raiding party across the river Scamander, where it flowed close under the heights of Mount Ida, some distance from Troy. He and his men were heading for the town of Lyrnessus, to the west. They waded through the shallow head-waters of the river, advancing with great caution in case scouts from the town were out searching for them. They had learned long ago that spies were everywhere about the country, marking their every move and spreading the word, so that it was difficult to keep any expedition secret for long.

On the further bank they ran into a small group of men who were returning to Troy after gathering firewood on Mount Ida. Achilles and his men quickly overcame them and their leader revealed himself as none other than Lycaon, a son of Priam. Achilles spared his life, but later sold him as a slave.

The cattle of Lyrnessus were spared that night, but shortly afterwards Achilles mounted an attack on the town itself, which was one of the last in the area to hold out against the Greeks. Lyrnessus was razed to the ground. Among the spoils of war which Achilles and his soldiers brought back to their camp were two girls whose beauty rivalled that of Aphrodite herself, Cryseis and Briseis. It was hard to say which of the girls was the more beautiful but Agamemnon who, as

commander of all the armies, had first choice in the share-out of any booty, chose Cryseis without hesitation and took her to share his tent. Briseis was given to Achilles.

Not long after this, a strange sickness spread through the camp. It grew worse day by day until soon the men were too weak to fight and many died in their tents. Small groups went out to look for healing herbs but none of the medicines they made from these had any effect on what had now become a serious plague. Agamemnon summoned a seer for advice. 'Mighty king,' the old man said, 'a great wrong has been done and the gods are angry.'
'In what way have we offended?' Agamemnon asked.
'You have in your tent a girl whom you have made your slave,' said the seer. 'She is a priestess of Apollo. In his fury he has sent this pestilence down upon you.'

Agamemnon was greatly troubled by this news, for he knew that priestesses were sacred to the god they served and that it was forbidden for men to touch them.
'What you say must be true,' he answered, 'but it was done in ignorance. How can we atone?'

The seer told him he must return Cryseis at once to her temple with gifts and sacrifices for the god. Agamemnon had no choice but to obey, though he did not wish to part from the girl. If he did not give her up, the Greek cause would be lost.

Grudgingly he released her, but immediately ordered Achilles to give him the other girl, Briseis, in her place. Achilles indignantly refused, but when Agamemnon ordered him as his commander he had to obey. Furious, he returned to his tent, swearing that neither he nor any of his men would play any further part in the war until Agamemnon had returned Briseis and apologized.

News of the quarrel soon reached Troy. Priam's soldiers grew bolder. New allies had recently arrived to support them and together they made a surprise attack on the Greek lines, pushing them back towards the sea and behind the wooden defensive walls they had built along the shore. The last man behind the barricades, still wielding his sword bravely, was Ajax, the captain of the Locrians. He left many dead behind him, but though Ajax was the hero of the day, the Greeks had suffered a severe defeat. There were murmurings among the men against Achilles.

Patroclus, Achilles's faithful friend, tried to defend him against the bitter words of the other leaders, but he knew in his heart that Achilles had not behaved as an honourable man and a soldier should. Agamemnon was at fault, too, but Patroclus could not influence him. He could, however try to persuade Achilles to stop sulking in his tent like a spoilt child.

'I will not stir until Agamemnon comes to me and begs for forgiveness,' answered Achilles.

Soon Patroclus's patience with his stubborn friend was near to breaking point.

'It seems to me that you have never left your childhood,' he said angrily. 'If I had not seen your braveness for myself, I should imagine you were wishing yourself back among the girls of Skyros!'

Even this taunt did not rouse the proud Achilles. Patroclus grew desperate to find a way of rallying the defeated, disheartened Greeks.

'Very well,' he said. 'Then I will take your armour and wear it on the field of battle, so that the Trojans will believe you have come to your senses, even if *I* know better.'

He took Achilles's helmet, shield, sword and spear and strode angrily from the tent. Achilles remained inside, brooding over his hurt pride.

The next day the Greeks swarmed back over their barricades, and the Trojans saw to their dismay the tall commanding figure of Achilles leading the soldiers forward. They fell steadily back towards the walls of the city and although Hector, their leader, urged them again and again to stand, the Greeks relentlessly pressed home their attack. Patroclus might easily have been Achilles from the way he fought: always in the thick of the battle, always spurring his men on, he was indeed a champion. By the time he reached the city gates, Hector alone barred his way forward. By this time, however, Patroclus had lost Achilles's helmet and could no longer conceal his true identity. Weary with hard fighting, he was no match for Hector and after only a short flurry of swords, Achilles's brave friend lay dying.

At full speed a Greek charioteer raced to Achilles's tent with the news. When he heard what had happened, the great warrior broke down and wept.

'Oh, that I should have done this to him!' he cried. 'My dearest friend sacrificed to my pride!'

He rose to his feet and strode from the tent. It was evening now and the Trojans were once more within their city walls. Achilles looked across the battlefield and saw in the distance Ajax and Odysseus lifting the body of Patroclus into a chariot to carry it back to the Greek lines.

In a voice like thunder he proclaimed: 'By all the gods, tomorrow will be a day of reckoning! For the memory of Patroclus a hundred – no, a thousand – men of Troy shall die!'

The very walls of the great city seemed to tremble under the darkening sky. For a moment

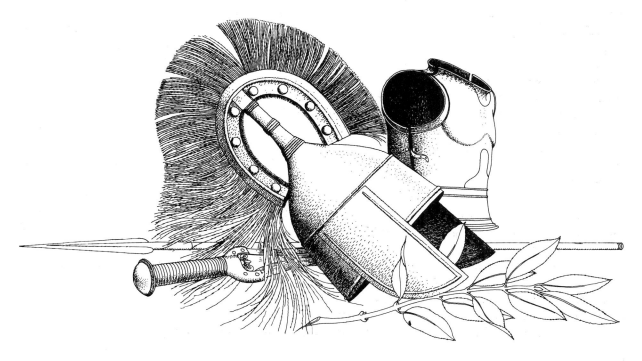

he stood gazing towards Troy, then went straight to Agamemnon's tent to make his peace.

Next morning the Trojans came out once more and another great battle was fought. Achilles and his men swept all before them. Their leader's figure seemed to tower above the rest and he wielded his sword like a great scythe, mowing down the enemy lines like corn at harvest time. The death of Patroclus had filled Achilles with an overpowering hatred for all the Trojans, a hatred only increased by the bitter knowledge that he himself had been the principal cause of Patroclus's death.

Under the onslaught of Achilles and his men, the Trojans moved back and once again they were fighting around the walls of the city. It began to seem as if this time the Greeks might finally overrun it, but one by one the gates were closed as the Trojan soldiers retreated to safety. Only the main gate remained open, defended to the last moment by Hector as his men rushed past him in disorder. As usual, Hector had led the Trojans with great courage throughout the day, but this time even he could not prevent the rout.

Achilles saw him from his chariot and hurled his spear with all his strength. The shaft would have pierced the very walls of Troy, so mighty was the force behind it. Hector fell with a deep wound in his neck.

'So shall all dogs die!' roared Achilles, leaping to the ground and rushing with raised sword at the fallen man. But Hector was dead by the time he reached him. Thwarted, and with his towering rage still upon him, Achilles tied Hector's feet with rope and fastening this to the back of his chariot, dragged the greatest of Priam's sons three times around the walls of Troy.

Such treatment of a fallen foe shocked even Achilles's friends, and brought a new fear to the Greek army. A dead warrior, friend or enemy, should be honoured with the proper burial rights, for without them he could never take his rightful place in the Elysian Fields. The wrath of the gods would certainly fall on the Greeks. However, when night came and they returned to their tents to rest and attend to the wounded, Achilles remained unrepentant.

'Let him lie as food for the vulture,' he said scornfully. 'Tomorrow we will watch them pick his bones.'

When the sun rose, King Priam looked out from the walls and saw his son's body still lying out on the plain. He called on Zeus for help and with the god's aid was able to disguise himself and make his way into the Greek camp unchallenged. When he reached Achilles's tent, he revealed who he was and threw himself on the Greek leader's mercy.

'In war,' he said, 'I know that many terrible things are done, things which in times of peace would never be imagined by sane men. But they are done in the heat of battle, without thinking and may, perhaps be forgiven in the end. I am an old man and have seen many things. But your treatment of the body of my dear son will be spoken of with horror and loathing wherever men of honour live. Your very name will stand for dishonour, and your triumphs will be forgotten. However, it is not too late to regain some of the respect which even we, your enemy, owe you. Let me take Hector back with me to the city so that he may have a proper burial and go in peace to Elysium.'

Achilles was moved by the old man's words. He was calmer now and knew that he had done a grave wrong. Nevertheless he was a proud man, and would not give way completely.

'You may take your son,' he said, 'if I receive his weight in gold in exchange.'

To this Priam agreed and a truce was declared for the day. A huge balance was brought from Troy and placed beside the walls near the gate where Hector had died. The Greeks lifted his body onto one side of the scale while the Trojans heaped gold from the vaults of Troy on the other. But the city had been impoverished by the long war and when all the gold had been brought out it did not quite tip the scale. Priam cast an anxious look at Achilles, but slowly the Greek shook his head. His terms had not been met.

However, someone had been watching the scene from the wall above – Hector's sister, Polyxena. When she saw her father turn away from Achilles, she at once took from her neck a heavy gold pendant and threw it down into the balance below. With its added weight, the scale shivered and swung downwards to balance exactly.

The Trojan soldiers carried Hector's body reverently away and Achilles, impressed by Polyxena's gesture, returned the pendant to her. Next day, the battle resumed as usual.

In the weeks that followed, Achilles found that he had fallen in love with Polyxena. Struggle as he might, he could not forget her face as she leaned down from the walls with her pendant; soon he knew that he could not live happily

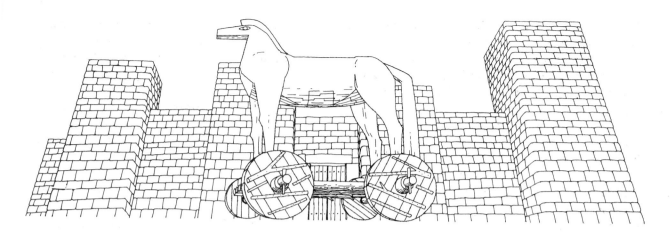

without her and he sent word to Priam that if he could have Polyxena for his wife, the war might be ended.

The Trojan king was overjoyed at the thought that the bitter struggle might at last be over and he arranged a meeting to discuss terms. Paris, however, was afraid that if peace came, he would be forced to give Helen back to her husband. As Achilles approached the city in peace he let fly a poisoned arrow. It struck Achilles in the heel, at the very spot where Thetis had held him so many years ago when she dipped him in the river Styx. The arrow's tip pierced his skin and the poison spread quickly. Slowly the tall figure sank to its knees to lie lifeless on the sandy ground.

After a brief moment of silent disbelief, a fanfare of horns sounded from the Greek lines. With Odysseus, Ajax and Diomedes in the lead, the massed chariots of the Greeks swept into the attack. The fighting that day was more bitter than ever before, and so it continued. As day followed day, it seemed that it would go on for ever.

Then, one morning, the Trojans looked out across the plain to find to their astonishment that the invaders had vanished. Nothing was to be seen but the last remnants of their empty camp. Even the ships had gone from the shore.

Outside the main gate of the city, mounted on a platform with roughly hewn wheels, was a gigantic wooden horse. On one flank the Trojans could make out an inscription dedicating the horse to the goddess Athene and praying for the safe return of the Greek armies to their homeland.

Cautiously, the Trojans inspected the horse, tapping it with their spears to test its construction and examining it from every angle. At first they suspected some kind of trick, but the horse, towering above them in the bright sunlight, did not appear to offer any threat. It was, they

decided, no more than it seemed, an offering to the goddess Athene, who had taken their side so often in the long war. After some discussion, the Trojans decided to bring it into the town, where it could stand as a fine monument to their un-expected victory over the Greeks. To leave it on the plain would be an insult to the goddess. They tied strong ropes about the base and pulled the horse through the streets to a wide square near the palace.

Day turned into night and for the first time in many years there was feasting in Troy. Around the wooden horse there was dancing and singing, and it was long past the middle of the night when the last of the revellers was asleep. Beside the city gates the guards, too, slept, heavy with wine.

When all was quiet at last, a secret trap door in the belly of the great horse slid noiselessly open. Fifty of the most daring of the Greek warriors dropped to the ground. Some of them ran at once to the gates; others crept towards the royal palace. Odysseus's cunning plan had worked out just as he had intended.

While the Trojans had been claiming the horse for their own, the Greek fleet had been sheltering out of sight in an island harbour nearby. As soon as night fell they had returned as swiftly and as silently as the wind and by the time the soldiers inside the city had killed the sleeping guards and opened the great gates, the army was massed on the plain. Once the enemy was inside the city, the Trojans were lost: completely unprepared, they fought their last battle. Before dawn came, the city had fallen to the Greeks, many of its greatest warriors were killed and their wives and children carried into slavery.

As for Helen, the cause of ten years of war and the death of so many heroes, she returned once more to her husband and to Greece.

The wanderings of Odysseus

After Troy had fallen, the Greek armies did not all sail back to Greece together. Once their common purpose was achieved, some of the commanders separated from the rest and went their own way. The journey from Troy to Greece does not look a long one on a map, but it was a journey full of dangers, especially when gods and monsters played a part. Odysseus, whose plan had brought about the fall of Troy, took many weary years to reach his home in Ithaca.

Odysseus and his ships sailed first of all to a part of Thrace called Circones, which lay to the west of two great rivers, the Hebrus and the Ergines. Here, their landing was opposed by the inhabitants of the district and the Greeks were forced to take to their ships without loading up the supplies and water they had hoped to find. They had intended to follow the Thracian coastline on their homeward journey. In this way they would always be near to land and could run for shelter if necessary. But it was the season of rough weather. Gales blew them out to sea and for many days they ran before winds of almost hurricane force, fearing for the safety of their ships.

Odysseus's ship was separated from the rest of the fleet and soon he and his crew had little idea of where they were. At last the winds eased, the seas went down, and land was sighted. It was the coast of Libya, the country of the Lotus-eaters and Odysseus made a landing there to replenish his supplies of drinking water. Although they had been warned against it, some of his soldiers tasted the seed of the lotus, a magical bean which so confused the minds of those who ate it that they remembered nothing of their former lives. These men wandered off, not knowing where they had come from, caring for nothing but dreams, and Odysseus, afraid that others might be tempted, called the rest of his soldiers back to the ships and weighed anchor without delay.

Their next call was at the island of Sicily, home of the Cyclopes. These were giant men, wild and unkempt, who lived on human flesh. Each had one eye only, gleaming balefully from the middle of his forehead. The terrible Polyphemus, taller even than all the rest, was their leader. He was a son of Poseidon and a nymph, and in his early days he and his followers had lead a more peaceful life. They had worked in the island forge doing fine metalwork and making thunderbolts for Zeus, guided by the watchful smith god Hephaestus. But under the evil influence of Polyphemus they had abandoned their trade and now lived by preying on the towns and villages of the countryside, stealing corn and herds and frightening the people.

All of this was unknown to Odysseus, and when he and his men had landed they set out to explore. They climbed the steep hillside above the bay where they had anchored, making their way between the rocks and boulders that dotted the slope. Ahead of them was a low cliff and as they drew near to it they could see the opening of a cave. In front of it, some long-eared goats were grazing.

'Wait here,' Odysseus told his men, 'and keep out of sight.'

The men took cover behind the rocks while their leader went on alone, moving with great caution. Close to the cave he paused and listened, but there was no sound except the sighing of the wind across the bleak hillside. He was reassured, but nonetheless he drew his sword as he crossed the last few metres to the cave entrance and looked inside. At first it was too dark to make out anything, but as his eyes became accustomed to the gloom he could see that the place was empty. It was much larger than he had imagined from outside, but there was no sign that it was occupied. There was only a pile of bones in one corner, indicating that it had been, or possibly still was, the lair of a wild animal of some kind. If so, the animal was not there now. Odysseus and his men would give it a rough welcome if and when it returned.

Odysseus went out into the afternoon sunshine and called to his men. 'We will make this our camp until we can find a better one,' he said. 'Tomorrow we will look for a town or village and buy grain and oil and other provisions. For today, we could do worse than feast on goats' meat.'

The men set to work killing some of the goats and roasting them over a fire which they lit in the cave. They squatted in a circle round the fire as they ate hungrily: fresh meat was something they had not seen for many weeks. Evening was drawing in by the time they had finished and the light in the cave was fading fast. Then, with dramatic suddenness, it vanished completely. Foolishly they had posted no sentries and they had heard no sound. Now when they looked round to see why it had gone so dark, they saw the gigantic figure of Polyphemus blocking the cave entrance completely, his single eye glowing red in the light from their fire. He was a terrifying sight; even Odysseus was afraid, though he put on a brave show.

'Can it be, stranger, that we have inadvertently made ourselves free with your flocks and your home?' he asked. 'If so, you must pardon us, for we are strangers and it seemed the place was deserted.'

But the giant only grunted in reply. Then he turned and went outside once more. Odysseus sprang to his feet.

'Quickly!' he said. 'Before he comes back we must get . . .'. But he had no time to finish his sentence, for the cave mouth had darkened once again as Polyphemus came back, driving his flock of goats in front of him. Once inside, he pulled a gigantic boulder across the cave mouth so that it was closed completely. Then, ignoring Odysseus and his companions, he lay down on the floor. Soon his snores echoed through the cave like thunder.

As it seemed unlikely that any sound they made would wake him, the men began to talk together, though they kept their voices low.

'I have heard of giants such as these,' Odysseus said. 'It would seem that we are among the Cyclopes, which is not the happiest place to be.'

'Do they not feed on human flesh?' one of the sailors asked.

Odysseus nodded. 'So they say. But they may go several days between their feasting,' he told them. 'Just the same, only luck has saved us from being roasted on this fire. We must escape as quickly as possible, for who knows what to-morrow may bring?'

They crept quietly to the cave entrance, but try as they might, the gigantic boulder which blocked the opening could not be moved. Eventually they had to give up. They dared not attack the giant while he slept, for even if they did succeed in killing him, they would still be trapped.

An uneasy night passed. In the morning Polyphemus drove the goats from the cave and pulled the rock across the opening from outside. They saw no more of him that day. The imprisoned men passed each hour in dread. Another night must inevitably come and with it, who knew what horrors?

But while some of the men gave themselves up to despair, Odysseus was busy plotting and planning. After a while he thought of a possible way in which they could escape. He took a shaft of wood and after sharpening one end, hardened it in the embers of the fire. Then he hid it under a goat skin on the floor and settled down to wait with the others.

That night Polyphemus came back and behaved just as he had done before. He brought in the flock of goats, moved the great slab of rock across the entrance, and settled down to sleep. Perhaps he had already fed or perhaps the band of Greeks were just lucky to have been in the cave during a period of fast, but soon his snores rumbled through the cavern once more.

When he judged that the night was nearly gone, Odysseus crept quietly to where the wooden shaft was hidden. Taking it out from under the skin, he heated the point in the fire until its sharpened end glowed red. Before it had time to cool he had crossed the cave to the sleeping figure and plunged the glowing stake into Polyphemus's single eye.

With a great roar of rage and pain the blinded giant staggered to his feet. Helplessly he blundered about the cave, arms outstretched, trying vainly to find his attackers, as they dodged away, always managing to keep behind him. At length he gave up and felt his way towards the entrance to the cave. Once there, he groped for the boulder and pushed it aside, but he did not venture out. Instead he crouched waiting by the opening, his huge, hairy fingers curled like talons. Obviously he knew the men would try to escape as soon as they could, and he was ready to seize them as they tried to pass him.

Odysseus had briefed his men well. Already each had captured a goat and now, clasping the the long hair of the goats' sides, they hung underneath them as the frightened animals made for the open doorway. Hearing the skuffle of their hooves on the stone floor, Polyphemus began to feel about, but all his hands touched was the familiar hair of the goats' backs and he suspected nothing. One by one the goats trotted past him out into the open air, and with them went the men, to freedom.

They lost no time in scrambling down the hill to their ship. As they rowed clear of the shore and hoisted their sail, Odysseus, standing in the stern, raised his voice and cried:
'Farewell, blind giant! Know that it was not the gods who took your sight, but mere weak men whom you could have destroyed with one finger!'

At the sound, Polyphemus came out from the cave, the huge boulder with which it had been closed held high above his head.
'Farewell!' Odysseus called yet again. The giant turned to the direction of the sound and hurled the boulder with all his strength after the fleeing ship. Then he stumbled to his knees. The boulder fell short, but not much more than a boat's length from the ship's stern. The vessel rocked dangerously, but it soon recovered itself. The crew looked back to see Polyphemus, a lonely, helpless figure, kneeling on the hillside.

With the help of Aeolus, king of the winds, Odysseus sailed to within sight of his island home on Ithaca. Aeolus had tied up all the adverse winds in a goatskin, but thinking that it contained treasure, the sailors opened it up while their captain slept. Thus they were blown away from the shore again and swept far to the west. At length they reached Aeaea, an island ruled by the goddess Circe. She had a reputation for disliking mankind and Odysseus sent a group of about twenty men to spy out the land before attempting to find food or water.

A man by the name of Eurylochus was chosen to lead the party. At first the goddess seemed friendly enough. But there was a look in her eye that Eurylochus did not care for and, when she invited the visitors to a feast, he sent the others but waited outside himself, watching. It was as well that he did so, for no sooner had the men sat down than Circe cast a spell over them which turned them into pigs.

Eurylochus made his way stealthily back to the ship and told his leader what had happened. Faced with an enchantress such as Circe, it was difficult even for Odysseus to know what to do. He was about to set out to attempt a rescue, armed only with his sword, when Hermes appeared. The god told him that he could be protected against Circe's spells by the white flower of a magic herb called moly which grew on the island. Armed with blooms of this herb Odysseus faced the goddess, and when her spell failed to work on him he threatened her. She begged for mercy.

'Only if you release my men will I spare you,' he told her. Instantly the pigs became men once more. Nevertheless, Circe was reluctant to let the party go, for she had fallen in love with Odysseus and wanted him to become her consort. He stayed on for a while, anxious though he was to be on his way, for he suspected that she might well have other powers to harm them. He avoided angering her, but left her in little doubt that he did not wish to stay for ever. Eventually she promised that he and his men would be released if they went first to the Underworld. There he was to consult the seer Teiresias, who would tell him what the future held. If he said that Aeaea should be their home they must abide by this, but Odysseus must return in any case to tell the goddess what the answer had been.

In the Underworld, Odysseus rejoiced at meeting many of his old comrades, but the news from Teiresias was not encouraging. Though he would eventually reach Ithaca in safety, he would find that in his absence others had seized his lands and property. Even now they were fighting among themselves about who should have the largest share of the spoils.

Their mission to the Underworld completed,

Odysseus and his men sailed back to Aeaea as they had promised. Fortunately, Circe kept her part of the bargain and did not oppose their departure. She even warned them of some of the perils they might encounter on their voyage and told them how these might be overcome.

First they had to pass the rocky coast where the Sirens lived. These creatures used to lure sailors from their ships with their singing. Their voices were so beautiful and their songs so haunting that anyone who heard them plunged to their deaths in the waves to remain near them. Following Circe's advice, Odysseus ordered his men to stop their ears with wax so that they could not hear the singing. He himself had heard so much about their music that he was determined to listen, but he made his men lash him fast to the mast, so that he could not escape. Even if he pleaded with them for his freedom as they sailed by, they were to take no notice.

In this way Odysseus and his men sailed past the Sirens and Odysseus became one of the few men to hear the Sirens' song and live. 'Though at the time,' he later said, 'I would gladly have sacrificed my life for the sound of their voices.'

Ahead lay further dangers. They had to pass through a narrow channel between towering rocks where the monsters Scylla and Charybdis lay in wait, like the Sirens, to trap passing ships. As the ship went by, Scylla, a six-headed monster, reached out her long arms and, uttering a curious yelping sound, clawed six sailors from the deck and devoured them. Odysseus altered course quickly, but in doing so steered perilously close to the great whirlpool of Charybdis.

Several times a day Charybdis would suck huge quantities of water into her enormous mouth and then spew it out again, so that the channel between the rocks seethed and whirled, drawing down into the depths even the mightiest ships which came within range. However, the wind was strong and the men pulled for their lives with the oars; they felt their stern dragged round and for several long minutes it seemed that they, too, would be sucked down. Somehow, however, they passed safely through.

Saddened by the loss of their six comrades, they rowed on. As they passed Sicily once more they found that their drinking water was again running low. They turned in towards the island and anchored in a cove well away from the place where the Cyclopes lived. They were now in the part of the island ruled by the god Helios.

Odysseus warned his men to behave peaceably, and not to take anything. They had, he said, had troubles enough. However, the sailors had already seen cattle grazing nearby and the prospect of eating fresh meat was a temptation they could not resist. While their leader was sleeping, they killed and roasted some cattle from Helios's herds. The god was outraged and, complained to Poseidon. He in turn had not forgiven Odysseus for blinding his son Polyphemus and when the ship sailed again he called up a wild storm. The ship foundered and everyone but Odysseus himself was drowned.

It was only because he was a strong swimmer that Odysseus was able to save himself. He managed to lash together fragments of wreck into a raft, but for many days he drifted helplessly before the gale, cold, hungry and with no fresh water to drink. The storm carried his raft back to the perilous channel where Scylla and Charybdis waited and this time his frail craft was sucked deep into the whirlpool. Odysseus struggled desperately to save himself, the rush of the waters filled his ears and spray almost blinded him. Death was very close. Then, as his raft was tossed up again in the centre of the whirling water, he stood upright and managed to grab at a fig tree which grew out of the cliff side. He pulled himself up onto this just as the raft vanished from sight. Then the gaping mouth of Charybdis closed, and the rushing waters became calm. Odysseus saw his chance and, dropping quickly from the tree, he swam to safety, out of the whirlpool's reach.

However, it was only a comparative safety for he was now far from any friendly shore; exhaustion could easily have proved more deadly than the twin monsters. Fortunately, the white goddess Leucothea came to him disguised as a seabird. In her beak she carried a veil which she told Odysseus to wind about his waist. Wearing this, he would never drown.

His journey was now nearly done. Helped by the veil, he was carried to the shores of an island, where he was found by Nausicaa, daughter of King Alcinous. He told her the story of his adventures, and the king gave him passage on a ship which was bound for his own island of Ithaca. When he reached it, he was sleeping. The sailors did not like to disturb his rest, so they carried him gently to the beach and left him there.

But though he was home at last after so many years, there were still troubles in store. Presently

he woke up to find the goddess Athene beside him. 'The seer Teiresias predicted that you would return unharmed,' she said. 'That much has been achieved satisfactorily. But remember that he also said other things.'

'That my possessions would be in the hands of others. Is that what you mean?' Odysseus asked. 'There should be little difficulty in dealing with them once I reveal myself. But what has happened to my wife Penelope? How has she survived in all this? And my son Telemachus?'

'Telemachus has gone to Sparta to try to gain some news of you from Menelaus and Helen, who recently returned from Troy,' Athene said. 'He has been powerless to stop what has been happening, for your enemies have been many and powerful, and indeed they are at this moment plotting to kill Telemachus on his return. In this way they hope to destroy the last protector of Penelope. She has waited faithfully for you. Many men have tried to persuade her into marriage, but with her son's help she has refused them all. They are all persistent and some have threatened violence, but she has held them off by promising that she will accept one or other of them when the tapestry she is weaving is complete. Each day she works at it and each night she unravels what she has done. But such a stratagem cannot succeed forever, particularly if Telemachus is taken from her.'

As he listened, Odysseus's anger grew. 'This must stop at once!' he cried. 'I do not fear these suitors, even if there are a hundred of them!' He drew his sword purposefully.

But Athene advised caution. Even if he did succeed in killing all the men who were against him, he perhaps did not realize how the long years away had changed him. Could he be certain that his wife would not turn away from him, thinking that he was simply another stranger seeking her hand and fortune?

Odysseus listened to what the goddess said and knew that she was right. A few more days' delay would make little difference. Athene suggested a plan. First, he let her turn him by magic into a tattered, bent old man, with white hair and a shambling gait. Then the goddess took him to the hut of Eumaeus, a shepherd who had worked for Odysseus before the war. She also sent Telemachus hurrying back from Sparta to join him there, guiding him around the trap which had been set for him by Penelope's suitors. Athene allowed Odysseus to return briefly to his true form, and the two men were let into the secret. But Telemachus, seeing a much older man than he remembered, had doubts, which proved how wise the goddess's caution had been.

'All Ithaca is certain that my father must have perished,' said Telemachus. 'I would gladly believe that this is not so, but how can I be sure that this is not one more plot to bring about the complete downfall of our family?'

At that moment they heard a sound from the door and, looking round, saw an old staghound with a grizzled muzzle come slowly through it. Many was the time in his younger days that he had hunted with Odysseus. At the sight of his master, the old dog's ears pricked up and his legs seemed to take on an extra spring. He came straight to Odysseus with his tail wagging and rubbed affectionately against him. Telemachus had no further doubts, but Athene advised that for the moment the news should be kept from Penelope. She might not be able to hide her joy from the people who crowded round her all the time and it would be best if she continued to behave exactly as before.

Back in the disguise of an old man, Odysseus went with Eumaeus and Telemachus to the palace to look around and see things for himself. There, the usurping nobles were eating and drinking and making free use of all Odysseus's possessions. When Odysseus appeared they laughed at him and made him the butt of their jokes, showing no sign of the respect that was due to an old man. Penelope, sad-faced and resigned, sat among them, and Odysseus knew that for her sake he must be patient and take their insults without reply.

The nobles were so sure of their power that they no longer kept their weapons with them as they feasted. The swords and spears were stored in an anteroom and the first thing Odysseus did was to instruct Eumaeus to remove them and hide them in the bushes in the garden. The nobles noticed nothing, and the feasting continued as one suitor after another tried to persuade Penelope to marry him. At first she was as firm as before, but perhaps even she was growing weary of the never-ending struggle. There seemed to be signs that she was beginning to waver and, seeing this, Telemachus spoke.

'If any of you men seek to supplant my father Odysseus, you must prove that you are at least as skilled as he with the bow,' he said to the assembled company. Perhaps Penelope heard something in her son's voice which gave her hope, or perhaps she simply knew that he must have a good reason for speaking like this.

'A reasonable condition, and I agree,' she said. 'He that can shoot an arrow with Odysseus's bow through no less than twelve axe-rings shall have my hand.'

The next morning the contest began and one by one the suitors tried to string and draw the bow. It was, however, so stout that they could not even bend it and their faces reddened with exertion and shame. Each new man was determined to show up those who had gone before, but at length all of them had tried without success. The last man threw the bow from him in disgust and anger.

As he did so, there was a stir from the back of the watching crowd and it parted as the white-haired old man they had mocked so pitilessly hobbled through. They jeered at him again as he picked up the bow, but the jeering soon turned to a murmur of wonder as the old man bent it easily. Stringing an arrow, he let it fly straight through the twelve axe-rings which had been placed upright in the ground.

For a long moment there was silence. Then the old man straightened and suddenly Odysseus was standing there. No one doubted now that this was the king. As one man, the suitors turned and rushed to the anteroom. By the time they had discovered that their weapons had vanished, Odysseus and Telemachus were attacking them, their swords whirling around their heads. Many fell mortally wounded; the rest ran away.

Odysseus was home.

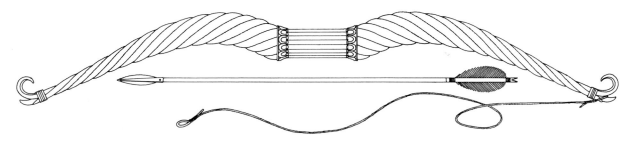

Symbols in the Greek myths

The original Greek gods were personifications of natural phenomena and were closely associated with different aspects of the countryside. Each animal, plant and natural feature was linked with one or more of the gods. In time, man-made objects also became identified with different gods, showing their special skills and responsibilities. At the beginning of each chapter, Giovanni Caselli has illustrated some of the symbols which traditionally represent the nature and adventures of the gods and heroes.

P.II THE WORLD OF THE GODS
The nature of Greece from Mount Olympus to the sea. The gods were involved in every aspect of man's life.

P.2I HADES, LORD OF THE UNDERWORLD
Black cypresses were associated with death and peace and are still found in cemeteries in Mediterranean lands. They were sacred to the death goddess Hecate, who was once the moon goddess. The three-headed dog is Cerberus, watchdog of the Underworld. The ferryman is Charon, who carried the souls of the dead from the land of the living.

P.25 PERSEPHONE AMONG THE DEAD
Demeter was the goddess of harvests and of all living plants. She is shown here with ears of wheat, olives and vines. The flowers are pomegranate flowers: it was because she ate seeds from a pomegranate that Persephone had to live for six months of the year in the Underworld.

P.29 POSEIDON'S OCEAN KINGDOM
Poseidon was the god of the oceans and of all marine creatures. Here, as well as different types of fish and shells, are some of the mythical sea beasts from his kingdom: a sea-horse and a triton.

P.33 PROMETHEUS AND PANDORA
Prometheus gave man fire, which he carried from Mount Olympus in the stalk of a giant fennel plant (bottom). Fennel stalks are still used today to carry fire. The wild orchid of the mountains was associated with Pandora (top).

P.37 APHRODITE, GODDESS OF LOVE
Aphrodite was associated with seas and shells. She rose from the sea on a scallop shell and one, *Venus callina*, was eaten as an aphrodisiac. Triton shells were offered to her in her temples. Doves are symbols of love, sparrows of lechery. Flowers sprang from the soil where she walked, symbolizing springtime, the season for love.

P.4I ARES, GOD OF WAR
The symbols of war: helmet and armour, spears, sword, bow and arrows.

P.44 ARTEMIS AND APOLLO
Apollo was the god of music and the arts. The figure at the top is Marsyas the satyr, who lost a contest with Apollo. The seven-stringed lyre is Apollo's special instrument; the laurel crown was traditionally awarded to poets and musicians. The flowers are poppies. At the bottom is a tripod used by Apollo's priestess at Delphi to deliver the oracle.

P.53 ATHENE, GODDESS OF WISDOM
Athene's principal symbols were the scales of justice, the owl — traditionally a wise bird — and the many objects she is believed to have taught man to make and use: earthenware pottery and (p.54) plough, rake, ox-yoke, chariot, ship, weaving and spinning, flutes and trumpets. She was also the goddess of just wars and patron of the city of Athens.

P.58 HERMES, THE MESSENGER OF THE GODS
When Hermes became Zeus's herald he was given a round hat, winged sandals and a herald's staff with white ribbons. He is said to have invented pan-pipes and the method of fortune-telling by throwing knuckle bones (bottom right).

P.60 PAN AND DIONYSUS, THE WILD GODS
Pan was the god of the countryside and of shepherds. The land of the pine and the oak was Dionysus's world, and a pine-cone formed the tip of his ivy-twined staff.

P.62 THE LABOURS OF HERCULES
Hercules always wore the skin of the Nemean lion (top) which he overcame in his first labour. The twin serpents are those he strangled in his cradle. Bow, arrows, sword and club were his favourite weapons.

P.73 THE ADVENTURES OF PERSEUS
The head of the gorgon Medusa could turn people to stone even after the monster itself was dead. It was often used as a decoration on shields — called a GORGONEION.

P.80 THE RIVAL TWINS
Castor and Polydeuces, the Dioscuri, were famous athletes. Polydeuces (top) was patron of boxers, Castor was a tamer of horses. After their death their images formed the constellation Gemini. Pear flowers and fruits are associated with them.

P.85 JASON AND THE GOLDEN FLEECE
Jason's adventures in search of the golden fleece (centre) involved him in a fight with the harpies (top). He was helped by Medea (bottom), a witch-princess.

P.97 THE HOUSE OF THEBES
Cadmus, the founder of Thebes, and his wife Harmonia, turned into serpents in their old age. After this time, all members of the ruling family were said to bear the mark of a snake on their bodies.

P.103 THESEUS, KING OF ATHENS
Theseus was a great king and warrior. His most famous symbols commemorate his fight with the minotaur (top) in the maze at Knossus (centre).

P.113 ORPHEUS AND EURYDICE
Eurydice's symbols are the leaves and fruits of the woods, for she was a wood nymph. The alder tree which grows on river banks represents Orpheus, whose lyre forms the background to the illustration.

P.119 EROS AND PSYCHE
Psyche, literally 'the soul', is now the name of a species of butterfly. Eros is known by his bow and arrows (bottom).

P.124 ECHO AND NARCISSUS
Narcissus's symbol is the flower which bears his name. He is also associated with the iris.

P.129 THE DEATH OF THE CHIMAERA
The story of Bellerophon involves the flying horse Pegasus (centre) and the Chimaera (bottom). At the top is the fountain of Hippocrene, where Bellerophon found Pegasus.

P.133 THE FALL OF TROY
The weapons of the period: helmet, bronze body armour, sword and shield, greaves or leg armour. The horse represents both the tough chariot horses and the wooden horse which tricked the Trojans at the end of the war.

P.144 THE WANDERINGS OF ODYSSEUS
The black circles represent the phases of the moon — time passing during Odysseus's long journey. The crab stands for the dangers of the unknown shores he came to. His wife Penelope (centre) symbolizes faithfulness. Odysseus's old dog recognized his much changed master (bottom). The bow and arrows proved his identity.

Index

Figures in italics refer to
colour illustrations